SAGE SLEEP

Rested and Connected

Rachel Rainbolt, M.A., CEIM

The Sage Parenting Series

1. Sage Parenting: Honored and Connected
2. Sage Sleep: Rested and Connected
3. Sage Breastfeeding: Nourished and Connected
4. Sage Homeschooling: Wise and Connected

Written by Rachel Rainbolt, M.A.
Edited by Casey Ebert, M.F.A.

Disclaimer

I recommend that parents consider options and become as informed as is possible, matching what you learn with what you think can work the best for your child(ren), you, and your family. You must use your wisdom and discretion in deciding what is in the best interest of your chi d(ren). The material in this book is meant to be considered in this process, providing relevant information, perspective, anecdotes, tools, and techniques for your inspiration and consideration. The products and product considerations recommended in this book are personal preferences. You are encouraged to investigate and form your own opinions as to the rightness of fit of any product for your child and you. The information in this book is not meant to be considered medical or psychotherapeutic advice. Rachel Rainbolt, Sage Parenting, is not liable or responsible for the parenting choices you make, actions you take, or any consequences thereof.

Copyright @ 2016 Rachel Rainbolt
All rights reserved.
ISBN-10: 1533394709
ISBN-13: 978-1533394705

DEDICATION

This book is dedicated to the four people whose love I breathe in all night long: Joshua, Sky, Bay, and West. Resting in bliss with these boys restores the strength and peace of my soul every night.

Contents

1	Sleep Baggage	8
2	Sleep Geography	22
3	Sleepscape	37
4	Sleep Routine	48
5	Sleep Neglect	65
6	Sleep Interrupted	73
7	Sleep Weaning	86
8	Day Sleep	91

INTRODUCTION

It's 3 a.m., and while the rest of the world is in a peaceful slumber, you are . . . not. You are up, half dressed, pacing vigorously up and down the hallway with a crying baby in your arms. Your hair is in your eyes, which are bloodshot, dry, and burning. As your body aches with fatigue and your nipples throb, your heart aches more for the sadness pouring out of this little extension of yourself. You are hearing all of those advice-givers in your head telling you that, "You will spoil them if you hold them too much"; "If you don't leave them in their crib, they will never learn to sleep through the night"; "If you pick them up every time they cry they will only cry more." You are just reaching a new level of desperation in your fatigue when your pacing lands you in the doorway to your bedroom. Your eyes fall on your partner, who is in perfect sync with the rest of the world, sleeping peacefully. That's it. You put the baby alarm right in front of his face and say, "Your turn!" as you walk out of the room for a breather.

I am going to give you the secret to sleeping through the night: don't have a baby! Parenting is a 24-hour job. Their needs don't stop just because the sun goes down. We've all been there. Everyone who has ever had a baby has been there. And in our zeal to be the best parent we can be, combined with the exhaustion a new mother faces, we try to impose all these ideas of what nighttime should be on ourselves: the picture of a baby sleeping soundly in a perfectly designed crib in a perfectly outfitted nursery, your mother-in-law telling you the only way to get any sleep is to let them "cry it out," maybe even your pediatrician warning you that whatever you do, don't bring your baby into your bed. Not to mention, "The amount your child sleeps is the yardstick by which other parents judge not only your parenting skills but also your child's development."[1] It is so important to enter parenthood and approach nighttime with appropriate expectations. I'm sorry if I'm the one breaking it to you, but newborns are not supposed to sleep through the night.

So what can a new family do to achieve a peaceful night? Well, the first step is to change the goal for nighttime from sleeping through the night to *harmony*. Nighttime harmony is priceless. It is the experience of being peacefully in sync with your baby throughout the night.[2] It is the difference between fighting against your baby in a battle for sleep and being connected with your baby for the mutual goal of rest.

1

SLEEP BAGGAGE

"You shouldn't hold a baby too much or you'll spoil them."

"You shouldn't breastfeed longer than a year."

"Good babies sleep through the night."

Every new parent comes to the table with baggage full of other peoples' truths. Loving family members, close friends, and well-meaning strangers (even the media) all fill your suitcase with what they think you should and should not do in the form of beliefs, assumptions, and expectations. Identify your baggage, let go of all that does not serve you, incorporate what does, leave space for new knowledge, and set your filter. If you don't shine a light on these other voices within, they will whisper in your ear in your most vulnerable moments and undermine your wisdom. *You are the world's foremost expert on your baby.* Listen to your innate wisdom. Release yourself from worrying about what's "right" and do what feels right for you and your baby.

We are formed through a combination of our DNA (nature) and our experiences (nurture). These things combine to form our personalities, points of view, and the foundations for our relationships. Our world is formed through a process of meaning making. An event occurs, we assign it meaning, and we internalize it. The way you were parented, your culture, your education, and all the way down to the disapproving glance you received from a fellow patron during lunch when your baby was crying, all form a network of meaning in your brain that lays the groundwork for how you interpret future experiences. Problems (or opportunities) occur when we experience dissonance, when something we know or assume to be truth collides with something else that feels right. When we are actively learning something new, this process takes place on more of a conscious level. For example: you are becoming friends with someone you were told was bad news. Who is wrong? What does it mean about the person giving the warning, your new friend, you, the world? As you grapple with these questions you reorganize your network of meaning, your understanding of the world and the people in it. But when we are not expressly setting out to accommodate new information, new feelings, truths, and experiences can lie in conflict with preexisting paradigms, thus creating dissonance. If we leave these conflicts battling inside us, we can drown in our own misguidance.

Entry into parenthood is a particularly exciting and

changing time. In transitioning from individual to parent, your experiences of parenthood from your parents and observations out in the world collide with your natural parenting instincts and intense bond and relationship with your new baby. Many new parents say that after the birth of their first child, the whole world was different. This is a result of this process of accommodation. Once you become a parent, your baggage or network of meaning is open to new interpretation. In other words, you see things in a whole new light.

Identify your baggage.

Picture a sweetly sleeping baby. Now zoom out.

> Where is a baby "supposed" to sleep?
>
> How "should" babies fall asleep?
>
> What does a "good" child do for sleep?
>
> What does a "successful" nighttime parent look like?

Take some time to walk through this hypothetical reality. Sit in the middle of it. Shine a light on every detail. Take notes without editing—let it flow. This is your *nighttime* parenting baggage.

Now let's find the origins of this baggage. Pulling back the curtain to see what is behind your assumptions takes away their power and frees you to make informed choices that are right for your specific little one. Next to each note you made, write down where it came from. Possibilities include:

- Things your parents did that you want to emulate.
- Things your parents did that you want to avoid.
- Baggage your co-parent brought to the table.
- Things your friends do with their children.
- Things your pediatrician told you to do.
- Things you read in a book.

This is the script you inherited from society, your upbringing, your friends, the media, etc. If you fail to achieve restfulness within the picture, you feel like a failure. Your child (and their natural needs) is not the problem. You are not the problem. The baggage, or the expectation, is the problem.

We are using nighttime parenting baggage as a starting point, but I encourage you to engage in this process with all types of baggage—from education to spiritual beliefs to discipline—with questions like:

> What is a "good" parent?
>
> What does a "well-behaved" child look like?
>
> How do children learn?

Let go of all that does not serve you.

We've identified your nighttime parenting baggage. Now we have to let go of all that does *not* serve you.

> Does this belief/assumption meet my little one's needs?
>
> Does this belief/assumption enhance my connection with my little one?

Which of your beliefs/assumptions/expectations do not serve you or your child? As you call them out or write them down, you are pulling them out of you and *releasing them*. We are moving from automation to intention. This baggage will no longer be the measure of your success. Peace, connection, and rest will take its place.

Incorporate what does.

Write down each belief/assumption/expectation that *does* serve you or your little one. As you call out or write down each belief/assumption/expectation you are saying, "This is whom I choose to be as a parent for this little one." Remember, nothing is neutral! It either adds to your peace and joy or takes away from it, so be discerning.

>What kind of parent has your baby conveyed that they need?

>What does the current research show?

>What path brings your family the most rest, peace, and joy?

Leave space for new knowledge.

After purging so much clutter, you may feel an uncomfortable amount of space or not knowing. Take a moment to sit in that anxiousness, without judgment, until you feel okay. Resist the urge to fill the vacuum of space. Because having the space to not know is a tremendous opportunity for growth. (If you think you know everything, you learn nothing!) What does this new space leave you noticing, wondering, or not knowing? Embrace this new posture of openness to learning.

Set your filter.

What kind of person do you want to raise (what qualities do you want to nurture)?

What kind of (long-term) relationship do you want to have with your child?

The answers to these questions will be your guide moving forward. Anytime something new tries to get in your baggage, ask yourself: "Is this a step toward these or away from them?" No interaction is neutral; you are always stepping in one direction or another. Every single experience is a step on your journey that provides a fresh perspective. Embrace a balance of confidence and openness as you move forward.
If something makes you uncomfortable, don't turn away. Face it, then work to change yourself or work to change it. Discomfort is an opportunity for growth.

Dealing with unwanted advice

Don't you love when people passive aggressively criticize you through your baby? "Oh, poor baby, you are so cold. I know, you wish you had a warm blanket," says an older woman in the store. Strangers and extended family members who are not caring for your baby think they know exactly what your baby needs.

This is a common perk of parenting an infant. Your mother quips: "You're hungry! You need to be fed." You say to yourself: "Oh really? You gleaned that in the 20 minutes that you've been here? I have been feeding her 24 hours a day for the last two months. My breasts and I know when she is hungry better than you. Thank you very little!" You think: "Maybe she's right—is my daughter hungry? Do I really not know my baby?" You feel insecure. This unsolicited advice and passive aggressive criticism is usually well-meaning, but unwelcome. Comments made in this way can undermine your confidence as a parent, and since they are given with a smile, they can more easily slip past your defenses and plant a seed of insecurity, undermining a knowledge or relationship that may be functioning to perfection. You listen to your baby, and trust in that. However, we can't just bury our heads in the sand since interaction with others can open us to new knowledge and ideas that may genuinely help us to be a better parent. When you hear advice given this way, train yourself to automatically flip it to its direct meaning and run a quick check (we're talking one second devoted to this—tops). "Is my baby cold? No. She is on my chest and amply warmed by my body heat." "Is my baby hungry? No. She just ate and is restless in my mother's arms because she is tired and wants to be back at home on my chest in her safe and cozy nest."

If a stranger is offering the advice, you can shut down the line of communication with a firm, "Nope." The most common tactic in the face of unsolicited counsel from a stranger or acquaintance is the smile and nod. But beware: any therapist will tell you that smiling and nodding is an affirmation—an invitation to say more.

You might be thinking, "Stop talking," but they are hearing, "Talk more." I recommend simply not smiling and nodding. It will feel incredibly awkward at first but they will get the message pretty quickly without any direct confrontation.

If it is a family member who is frequently offering the unwanted advice through your baby, call it out for what it is in a respectful way. "I know you are speaking from a place of love for my baby and I appreciate that. If you have a concern about her care, please tell me directly and I'll let you know whether or not it is helpful. Rest assured that she is fed when she is hungry, so it is not helpful for you to suggest that she is hungry anymore." Or, "We have a great deal of respect for you and value the wisdom you have to share with us. We have considered what you have to say on this issue, done our own research, gotten to know our baby, and have decided that on this issue we are going to do X. You don't have to agree with our decision, but we ask that you do respect it."

Pediatricians can be indescribably valuable members of your village of support along your parenting journey. They can also be a heavy source of baggage bullshit. The system is set up in such a way that new parents seek permission, approval, and non-medical advice from pediatricians that is beyond their scope and distorts the reality of the relationship, perpetuating a grossly skewed power differential. *Pediatricians are not gods*; they are *medical* doctors and they work for you. Did you know that pediatricians receive virtually no training in breastfeeding? Yet that does not stop nearly every mother from walking out of one of those well child visits being told how she "shouldn't" be nursing at night. The *parenting* advice they dole out, though prescribed with authority, is based on personal opinion, not medical science. So keep advice from your pediatrician in that context. *You* are this baby's mother and these decisions are yours to research, consider, and make. My recommended response filter is: "Based on what?"

> "By 8 weeks you should cease all night feedings. He no longer needs that and you are setting up bad habits. He is capable of sleeping through the night."
>
> "Based on what?"
>
> "Well . . . he just doesn't need it."
>
> "So you don't have actual medical science to support those recommendations? Do you have specific training in breastfeeding or nighttime parenting that informs that recommendation or is it just your personal opinion? We don't base our parenting choices on the uninformed opinions of others."

Think of the advice and expectations of those around you in your circle of support, including experts like me, like parenting tools: the more tools you know about, the better. You may not need one tool now, but it may come in handy to pull it out in some situation in the future. You can pick and choose which tools work for you for the task at hand. Some tools you know you will never use—discard them or they will only weigh you down. Remember: you can acknowledge that someone's advice is not right for you while still respecting the person from whom it came.

Unpack your baggage together.

Parenting differences is one of the top reasons for divorce in this country. Unpacking your baggage together is a superb way of getting co-parents on the same page, especially when unconscious allegiances with families of origin and conflicting baggage weigh heavily. A lot of our parenting choices are based on the choices of our parents, which we either seek to emulate or avoid. Some of their ideals and strategies may very well be worth emulation; when you think of them, you feel warm and fuzzy and recall particularly valuable growth. Others may very well be deplorable, even illegal, by today's standards. Coming together with your parenting partner to discuss your parenting strategies is essential to successful co-parenting. This process will take place periodically as new dissonances emerge, life events occur, and new developmental phases are reached. When unpacking your baggage with a partner, it is important to keep in mind that every child is different. What worked for you is not necessarily what is best for your child. Let this be the focus of your discussions. It is important to understand that just because your partner does not think a particular parenting strategy is right for your baby, that doesn't mean she thinks your mother's way was wrong.

Stay flexible. Revisit frequently. Respect permanent boundaries.

You may have agreed to a parenting strategy early on that needs to be adjusted. Things change, people change, and children change frequently. Perhaps in getting to know your child better you find a particular strategy is not effective. Perhaps in their new phase of development your previous strategy no longer works. Maybe your reentry into the workplace requires some adjustments on everyone's part. People are engaged in a process of growth throughout their entire lifespan. The idea is that people are striving to be better. In this growth, accommodations frequently need to be made and they are usually for the better. So stay open and be flexible. However, every parent usually has in his or her baggage a couple permanent lines they will not cross. For example, no hitting a child—ever, under any circumstances. If your co-parent has disclosed one of these items, be respectful of it and work together to find other solutions.

Don't unpack during a fight.

Sometimes you'll fight out an issue and come out the other side with a resolution. But more likely, you will be met with defensiveness, tangle more than one issue together, and cement your positions on opposite sides of the battlefield. There are a lot of good times to unpack your baggage: shopping at the grocery store, on a walk, over dinner, or in the car. But during a fight is not one of them.

Take your time.

Don't force a resolution in the moment. When a partner brings up a parenting issue, feel free to take time to sit with it. Really think about it, live it out in your head, research it, and ask around in your circle of support. This will help to avoid snap decisions or judgments. Even if you don't agree with everything your partner says, they will feel more respect if you genuinely give thought to their concerns. And wouldn't you want the same?

Be Respectful.

Some parenting traditions may seem pointless or foreign to you, but inheriting the combined culture of both parents most benefits your baby. As long as your partner's requests are not harmful, be open to them.

Be aware that in calling your husband's suggestion stupid (which he is basing on the way his mother parented him), he may be hearing, "I think your mom was a crappy mother." Be respectful not only of the entire conversation but of the origins of what your partner brings to the table.

Remember that this is about your baby.

Think of it like working together on your family's Christmas cookie recipe. You love that his grandma adds cinnamon. Your mom adds some nice flavor with vanilla. You had some cookies once at a friend's house that were superb because of her sugar to flour ratio. You once read in a cookbook that letting the dough sit before you bake brings out the best in all the secret ingredients. Last, and most importantly, your baby's favorite treat is powdered sugar and they are too young for chocolate. You select a non-chocolate cookie and heap spoonfuls of powdered sugar on top as the crowning glory.

My Journey

Up at 3:30 a.m. with my 1-month-old firstborn baby, I found myself . . . drowning. I was completely exhausted with no sleep and a parasite (albeit a cute parasite) whose days and nights were breastfeeding marathons with intermittent breaks to cry and spit up, only to work up an appetite and make room for more milk. It was in this moment, reaching my breaking point, when I realized that the tornado ripping me apart that night was not coming from my baby or anything else external, but from inside of me. A whirlwind of "shoulds" and "shouldn'ts" left me chipped away to nothing. "Good babies sleep through the night." "Don't hold him too much or you'll spoil him." "If you bring him into your bed, you'll never get him out." This tornado of foreign voices left me dizzy and disconnected from myself. It was in this place of desperation that I surrendered. I lay in my bed sobbing, white-knuckled, clenching the baby monitor when I surrendered, let down my walls enough to really hear my husband nonchalantly say, "If he wants you to hold him, and you want to hold him, why don't you hold him?"

Bam! There it was. My world was never the same. In that singular moment I realized that in my zealousness to do everything "right" I became lost, disconnected from my baby and myself. There is no way to win when you are held hostage by other people's truths. All of a sudden I could feel my own maternal wisdom swelling inside my heart like a wave, and I threw the monitor, ran to my baby, and allowed my love and wisdom to wash over both of us. "I am your Mommy. I know what's best for us." I empowered my voice. And as my relationship with my baby grew deeper and stronger every day, taking advantage of every moment as an opportunity to bond and researching long-held assumptions, beliefs, and expectations with an open mind, my identity as a mother grew stronger and more positive. Before long, I was glowing in harmony with my baby. My husband, listening to his innate wisdom as a father, provided me with the key I needed to unlock all of my internal wisdom and empower my maternal voice. I am forever grateful to my partner, spouse, co-parent, and best friend for setting me on the path toward reaching my potential as a mother, parenting coach, and human being.

Altogether

The point is not that you adopt my particular point of view but that you engage in the process of forming and empowering your own maternal voice. Recognize where your ideals come from, how they have been formed, and take into consideration your knowledge of your baby and your family along with the information available today, to form your own parenting principles.

2

SLEEP GEOGRAPHY

Sleep geography is the setting for your sleep story—the where. We're going to choose the room for sleep with intention, ditch the baby cage, and set up the right sleep surface for your family.

Room

Master Bedroom

Where do you and your baby sleep best? Contrary to popular belief, you are the most qualified expert to answer that question. Babies are born hard-wired to live on your chest (there they are content on their home base with their needs met quickly and easily), so evolutionarily, it makes the most sense to have a shared sleeping space. But many personal and experiential factors weave together to form the fabric of your ideal sleep geography. Connection-based sleep can be set up in almost any room of the house, so which room would be best for your family?

The room you have already designed for your sleeping comfort is the default family sleeping space. Research shows us that it is safest for your baby and allows you to meet more of their natural needs while remaining restful yourself. The biggest challenge here is usually just the nighttime parenting baggage and pressure from outside sources. Thankfully, we have already unpacked that baggage. If your partner is questioning where couple connection fits into this sleep arrangement, I encourage you to read the Sex After Baby chapter along with the Who Comes First chapter of the Sage Parenting book.[3] Co-sleeping (shared room or sleeping within sensory range of your child) does not inhibit independence. A little one who feels sleep is a time of security and love grows to embrace its comfort, not fear it.

Nursery

It makes sense to transition your little one to a separate bedroom when they express (child led) or you feel a desire for more nighttime space. For example, perhaps you and your sweet babe are both very light sleepers and your nighttime noises are now waking you both up throughout the night.

Cribs

Let's raise our children with at least as much respect as we want for the chickens we eat: cage-free. A crib-less nightlife is safe and yields more sleep and independence. So let's take a closer look at why we should banish baby jail.

Respect: You shouldn't do anything to your baby you wouldn't want done to you. Would you want to be jailed all alone in an empty cage?

Mama Sleep: If you have to get up to meet your baby's needs you will have less restful nights.

Child Sleep: Infants sleep best the way Mother Nature programmed them to sleep, over millions of years of evolution: with their loving caregiver. As they grow, sleep arrangements that honor the child's natural rhythms and balance of autonomy and connection foster a positive lifelong relationship with sleep. There is no opportunity for connection on a sleep surface in a crib.

Independence: Independence is not fostered in a sleep arrangement that leaves your little one completely dependent upon you to meet 100% of their needs (trapped in a box, unable to access the things, people, or freedom they might need).

Safety: Intentional co-sleeping is safer than crib sleeping. Floor beds set you up to teach your little ones to safely interact with their child-friendly environment, which is safer than attempting to barricade them from it.

Sleep Surface

When it comes to the actual sleep surface, you have

some flexibility in choosing an arrangement that most resonates with you while still fostering that connection and independence. You'll notice all of these sleep arrangements are a departure from the mainstream method of control and forced premature separation, and they all maintain a feature of permeability, wherein the connection is free to ebb and flow with the child's needs and blossoming independence.

Bed-Sharing

You are simply sharing a sleep surface with your baby. You bring your baby into your bed. It is the simplest and most natural of all the sleep arrangements.

That image of the perfectly decorated nursery is a nice one, but when it comes to actually sleeping, you have to be a little creative, open-minded, and accepting of whatever arrangement gives everyone the most sleep. Bed-sharing is something that some mothers come to unintentionally, out of a desperate need for more sleep. After waking up, walking down the hall, picking up Baby, nursing while sitting up in the rocking chair, and putting Baby back to bed, you think, "I'll just pick him up and bring him to my bed and nurse him there. That way I can lie down." You fall asleep nursing and realize, "Oh my god, I just slept four hours!" The reason bed-sharing works so well is because your baby is getting all the things that make them thrive: skin-to-skin contact, milk, Mom's breathing regulating their own, Mom's heartbeat as a soothing reminder of the womb, and Mom's chest regulating their temperature. And while Baby is in heaven, so is Mom. You do your job of meeting your baby's needs while lying and resting effortlessly in bed—talk about harmony. My baby and I breathed each other in and breathed out love for the other all night long. The warmth between us sparked the bond we lived on all day. Breastfeeding in bed requires some new positions, but they are totally worth mastering. The side-laying position is the classic bed-sharing arrangement. Lie on your side (you can put a pillow behind your back) and lay baby on their side or back, mouth to nipple. You can rest their head on your arm or not. My babies and I were lovingly and happily cuddled in perfect, restful harmony all night long.

Dads are sometimes unsure of how they will fare in this arrangement. Assure your partner that a happy, rested mama means a happier wife. Some dads end up spending the first few weeks or so on a separate sleeping surface to give Mom and Baby the space to figure out the physical aspects of bed-sharing without having to worry about Dad rolling onto the baby (my husband made a bed on the floor next to us in the very beginning with our first). With our second and third, we were all able to harmoniously sleep together in our big family bed from the beginning. A new baby takes work and sacrifice from both parents; Dad has to do his part too.

When moms bed-share with their babies, they are so sharply attuned to them that amazing things happen. If Baby moves their head back, Mom moves her head forward. If Baby scoots down, Mom scoots down. This is called molding. It's a remarkable testament to the connection between Mom and Baby. Mothers accommodate their baby's position all night long, and the slightest wiggle or disturbance on the part of the baby results in a hovering, awake mother. This is not true however, of fathers. Since fathers don't get to spend nine months tuning in to Baby, they are not attuned to them while sleeping in this special way. That's why Baby should sleep next to Mom. This attentive attunement is also not present if Mom has had any alcohol, drugs, or medication. Research also tells us that breastfeeding moms are especially tuned in to Baby, and this special relationship acts as a major protective force while co-sleeping.[3]

You should know that research absolutely supports the safety of bed-sharing.[4, 5, 6, 7, 8, 9] In fact, "Data from the Sudden Unexpected Deaths in Infants Study found that babies sleeping alone in a room were twice as likely to die as those who share a room with their parents."[10]

That said, there are some guidelines to maximize the safety of this sleeping arrangement.

1. Breastfeed
2. No big comforters pulled up near Baby
3. Mattress on the floor
4. No siblings in the bed
5. Baby sleeps next to Mom
6. No alcohol, drugs, or medications of any kind
7. Baby is put to sleep on their back

Common Misconception: *Co-sleeping increases the risk of SIDS (Sudden Infant Death Syndrome).* Research shows that the opposite is true.[11] When babies sleep next to an attached caregiver there are several factors at play working to protect babies against SIDS.

- Mother is tuned in to Baby for signs of distress.

- Baby mirrors Mother's steady and rhythmic breathing ("reminds" Baby to breath).
- Baby mirrors Mother's steady and rhythmic heart rate.
- The sucking from frequent breastfeeding increases brain activity and fluid production, as well as the flow and efficiency of all baby's systems.
- Skin-to-skin contact increases the level of feel-good hormones and decreases the level of stress hormones.
- Mother's chest actually regulates Baby's temperature. If Baby's temperature rises, Mother's temperature lowers. If Baby's temperature lowers, Mother's temperature rises and she expels heat from her chest to warm Baby.

Side-Car Crib

To co-sleep actually means to sleep in close proximity with baby. "Extensive scientific research shows that safe co-sleeping can be a real investment for your child's future physical and emotional health."[1] Co-sleeping, or sleeping within sensory range of your baby (you can see and hear your baby breathing), is actually the sleep arrangement recommended by the AAP[12]. It usually looks like a crib next to your bed. What I described above is bed-sharing, but co-sleeping can take other forms.

The side-car crib sleep arrangement can be nice if you already own a crib. You are setting up a sleep surface for your baby that acts as an extension of your own.

Assemble the crib in toddler-bed mode (remove the front rail and attach the small support), raise the crib mattress to the same height as your mattress, and pin the crib right between the wall and your bed. Then slide the crib mattress up against your mattress, and you can place a pool noodle or blocks of high-density foam in the gap between the crib mattress and the back of the crib.

Side-Car Bed

In placing a mattress alongside your own (between the wall and your mattress or floating in the room with a bed rail or bumper on Baby's side edge) you are creating one large shared sleep surface.

With both the side-car crib and side-car bed sleep surface arrangement, your baby will have their own designated space but be within arm's reach. This means you can hear every breath and all you have to do is open your eyes to see their little chest moving up and down. You can pull them close for nursing and cuddling and slide them back over to sleep.

Personally, this arrangement is actually my favorite as it allows for maximum connection and sleep while providing your little one the space to grow. I find that this provides the perfect balance whereby I can get the best sleep. If my baby is in a different room, I can't sleep. I worry about him and have to get up constantly to meet his needs. If my newborn is in my bed all night, I can feel like I am "on the clock" and have trouble reaching the deepest stages of sleep. But with my baby co-sleeping right next to me I can lie right next to him, nose to nose, all night long, pulling him over for breastfeeding/drowsing periods and sliding him back when I want some serious, deep sleep. Then as he grows, he is able to meet his needs (scooting close and even latching on his own when needed) and enjoy his independence (flopping around undisturbed in his own space). This is also the sleep arrangement that makes the most financial sense as you are purchasing one mattress that will last your little one's entire childhood. You know what they say about Attachment Parenting—it's great for the lazy and cheap. (Who wouldn't want more sleep and more money?)

Floor Bed

A floor bed (advocated in Montessori) is a sleep surface for your little one where the mattress is placed directly on the floor. If you and your child are ready for them to transition to a separate space, this is the only sleep arrangement I recommend.

Flexibility

It is also worth noting that sleep arrangements are fluid. For example, Baby may start out on their own sleeping surface for the first part of the night (their deepest and longest stretch of sleep is that first sleep cycle) and then bed-share the remaining portion of the night (which is typically marked by a high level of frequent need while drowsing). What sleep arrangement results in the most restful harmony for you and your baby? I encourage you to find the arrangement that works best for you. Every baby is different. Every mother is different. Every family is different. Do what works best for you and your baby.

As nighttime feedings fade, the picture of your nighttime sleep arrangement may evolve. Some families opt to transition away from co-sleeping as their child's sleep independence increases. Many opt to continue with what is the norm throughout most of the world: the intentional family bed. In Japan, for example, there is typically one sleeping room in which all family members dwell until adolescence, when the children naturally set out to establish their own independence.

In our master bedroom, we have had, at one time or another, a side-carred crib and a side-carred bed (a twin-sized mattress placed horizontally at the foot of our bed or one pulled up alongside our king-sized mattress (creating an extra-wide bed)). All have been heavenly. We have also had a split-level family bed with a low-profile bunk bed couched between our bed and the wall. The bottom mattress rested directly on the floor, placing our mattress height between the upper and lower mattresses. Our toddler slept on the bottom, and the top was for either or both of our bigger boys. It was amazing. Each boy had his own room with his own bed and a space to sleep in the family bed. The boys thought it was super cool and we loved it. It was the perfect sleep arrangement for our family at that time.

Fear of Sleep Dependency

The fear of fostering sleep dependency is a big one in the world of nighttime parenting. Can your bedtime routine consist of saying goodnight to your child and sending them off to bed? Sure. Is that in your child's best interest? Not likely. Many sleep problems associated with early childhood stem from prematurely forcing sleep independence on young children. As with all aspects of parenting, remember that little ones are dependent; they are supposed to be—that's why they have you. As they get older, allow them to lead the walk down the path of independence, including and especially with bedtime. If a child's needs for security and trust are met, they feel comfortable and confident to be more independent sooner. It may feel counterintuitive to pull a child in closer who is behaving in a way that you deem overly dependent, but that is precisely what you can do to ease any anxiety and provide the safe foundation from which to launch into independence. "We should *never* be scared of creating clingy children by allowing them to be dependent on us and fulfilling their needs, for fulfilling these needs is the very best way to create confident, independent individuals."[1]

Scientific research seeking negative outcomes of bed-sharing and co-sleeping consistently comes up empty. "Once the child was five years old their cognitive and behavioral functioning were tested, focusing on their hyperactivity levels and social skills. Unsurprisingly, those children who had regularly bedshared with their parents did not display any more problems than those who had not."[1] Another study found that "at age 6 years, bedsharing in infancy and early childhood was not associated with sleep problems, sexual pathology, or any other problematic consequences. At age 18 years, bedsharing in infancy and childhood was unrelated to pathology or problematic consequences."[13] These studies also illustrate the lack of long-term efficacy consistent with the warnings parents receive to sleep train their babies so that they will learn to sleep independently for the long haul. One study out of Switzerland "... found that at the age of four almost 40 percent of the five hundred children studied were sleeping in their parents' bed at least once a week. Interestingly, they also found that those who slept separately from their parents as a baby were no less likely to share a bed with their parents by the time they reached school age."[15] Whereas, "...children who had never shared their parents' bed were three times more likely to be overweight compared to those that shared a bed with their parents."[14] On the flip side, studies show ample long-term benefits to shared sleep in addition to the obvious short-term benefits including "... *greater* independence, *less* reliance on transitional objects, *less* thumb-sucking, and *greater* cognitive competence and psychosexual adjustment."[16]

Children don't mind sleeping. They don't even mind sleeping in their own rooms or their own beds. Children are afraid of sleeping alone and that is evolution at work. You want to know what evolution calls children alone in the dark? Food! Children who have a fear of being alone at night and a heightened sense of sound and movement in the darkness have always been more likely to survive! There seems to be a big emphasis on pushing babies and children to sleep alone. Understand that evolution has hardwired into your child's DNA a fear of being alone in the dark at night. The monster in your child's closet is a predator.

Our natural predators hunt at night and target the unprotected. From an evolutionary perspective, a child was much less likely to survive if they were alone and unafraid in the dark. A child who had a drive to elicit protection at night and who possessed a keen sense of sound and movement in the darkness would have been more likely to survive. Therefore this fear was selected for. In other words, children who possessed this fear didn't get eaten by a lion and lived to pass on their DNA. While some parents dismiss this very common and normal preference for being watched over and for a source of light, it does have a biological basis. In many cultures around the world it would be considered cruel to isolate your child in darkness.

> "How will your children learn the joy of solitary sleep?"

> "Oh, so you and your partner sleep alone in separate rooms?"

Do you prefer to sleep alone? All human beings have a strong desire, and even a physical need, for connection. I'm willing to bet that you prefer to sleep with your significant other. You might roll close for some physical contact to raise the levels of all those feel-good hormones and then roll back over to your side. Many parents have tried to kick their 5-year-old out of their room only to be met with, "*You* don't sleep alone." Busted. The point is not that you must expand your bedroom to include extra twin-size beds, but that you respect your child's requests for closeness and connection as reasonable and natural and attempt to meet those needs in ways that agree with yours, such as integrating high-touch components and allowing intimate interaction time in the bedtime routine. Just as you enjoy benefits of nighttime connection, it can help your child to flourish.

Habits seem to be the big scary monster in parents' closets that intimidate them into shying away from bedtime routines that are based on connection and revolve around closeness. Many parents are afraid that if they engage in an activity that feels good and works for everyone now, they will be stuck with that arrangement forever. It is true that if you do something over and over again, you may find yourself repeating it even after the need for it is gone. Your toddler may be in the habit of being carried everywhere. When it is time to go they may reflexively raise their arms to be lifted, but when they are ready, they will want to get down and walk and run . . . everywhere . . . all the time . . . even when you're in a hurry . . . or crossing a busy parking lot.

Habits are sometimes formed but they do not have the bite that parents fear. A habit will not prevent your child from moving down their path of independence. If you wake up one day and decide that an arrangement is no longer working for you, you can always change it with replacement, consistency, and reassurance. A habit can be broken or a nighttime ritual can be replaced in a matter of days. Fear of forming a habit is not a valid reason for missing out on harmonious experiences that are in everyone's best interest now.

"My 2-month-old son just does not sleep in his crib. He and I are both up for hours every night. When I brought him into our bed last night, we both finally got sleep! We breastfed a few times, but he didn't have to fully wake himself to a cry to get the milk, and I didn't even have to sit up to feed him. I feel so rested. But I do not want to bed-share. I don't want to start that habit."

So let me get this straight—you are going to spend the next year running on no sleep because you are afraid you will have a teenage boy who wants to sleep with his mommy? That would be like saying you are not going to hold your baby because if you do, he will never want or learn to walk. Preposterous! When he is ready, he will be tearing out of your arms to run away. Do what is right for you and your little one. If you employ an arrangement that fosters feelings of peace and security at nighttime, then your child will be less anxious and dependent than his peers. And if one day, before he transitions on his own, you decide that you are ready for him to begin the transition, you can do just that.

What if we extended that fear of habit-forming from nighttime to feeding? Would you not breastfeed or feed your baby from a bottle out of a fear that it could become a habit? Absolutely not, because you prioritize meeting the needs of your child now and trust that when they are ready, they will want food. If you do find yourself among the minority with a child who isn't ready to wean on their own but you are no longer willing to meet that need, you always have the option of weaning them. The same is true for nighttime. Rest assured that you can meet your child's needs now and they will continue to grow and develop, moving on to new arrangements and activities. And you always have the power to replace with a new routine. One day you will long for this precious time again.

Common Misconception: *Once you bring a baby into your bed, you will never get them out.* Ridiculous. As discussed above, a baby is dependent as an infant. Allow them a time of dependence! You will not have a 15-year-old in your bed. The more you give them what they need to feel secure as an infant, the more safe, secure, and confident they will feel to be more independent than their prematurely pushed counterparts. If you are worried about it, you can use a transitional strategy. Baby sleeps with you while they are breastfeeding during the night. You can then put their bed right next to yours (like an extension of your bed). You can then move their bed to the foot of your bed. Lastly, move their bed into their room. Include them in the process of selecting a bed and bedding and make it fun and positive. On a personal note, my firstborn son slept in our room when he was a baby. Even after he was done breastfeeding at night, my husband in particular liked him in our room. Since my husband worked all day, he valued the closeness that having him with us at night provided. One day he just asked for a bed in his room. We provided him with security and allowed him to take the lead in establishing his independence. We now have a son full of love, trust, inner peace, and independence. Now ten years old, he is lying in his bed, quietly and calmly reading a book on his own. He treasures our bonding time during his bedtime routine and then appreciates the independence that caps off his night.

There is absolutely nothing inherently wrong with enjoying a family bed. In fact, *this is the norm throughout most of the world*. If you are content, your child is content, and a family bed works for your family, then pull a twin mattress up alongside your king and enjoy it! If the only reason you have a nighttime "problem" is because of external pressure or shame based on arbitrary "shoulds" and "should nots," then you don't really have a problem at all.

3

SLEEPSCAPE

Now that we have settled onto the right branch, let's build our nest. We get to design the sleepscape that will foster a healthy, life-long relationship with sleep while meeting present needs. First we're going to strip it down, then we'll set it up, and finally, we'll make it safe.

Remove

Remove everything from the room except the mattress and the dresser. It is likely that many items have found their way into this sleeping space and they need to be purged, as we are going to invite any items in with the greatest of intention. Clear the space for a fresh start with a new perspective. Moving forward there will be nothing stimulating in the sleeping room (put all other toys and activities in a shared space where you will be awake and playing together).

Add

Invite into the space only things that add to the peaceful, calm, and restful energy of the room. The most important piece here is to think about all of the senses. Babies are sensory creatures and tapping into all of the senses is a huge piece missing from most approaches to sleep. Remember, nothing is neutral. It either adds to the sleepscape or it takes from it.

Touch

Bedding

In infancy, there should only be a fitted sheet on the mattress. Every additional item of bedding you introduce only serves to decrease the safety of the sleep surface. When selecting bedding you want to be mindful of what fabric is comfortable to your little one. (What texture do they find soothing?) Pillows and a blanket for your comfort can be set down just off the sleep surface of a floor bed when you are not in shared company with your baby or well out of their sleep zone if sharing the master bed (pillows well above their head and blankets well below their feet). Lots of pillows and blankets can be present in the space as your child grows. My Bay loves to build "nests" out of pillows and blankets and curl up right inside.

Pajamas

Be mindful of what fabric, tightness, and level of dress are comfortable for your little one. Some prefer to be swaddled in muslin while others prefer to sleep in nothing but a diaper. You can look to your baby's cues to get to know their preferences and then respect them in their level of dress.

Temperature

Around 72 degrees is a sweet spot for many but be mindful of what room temperature results in the best sleep for your little one. Some prefer warmer while some prefer cooler. Balance your little one's temperature preference with your own but keep in mind they are not huddled under thick blankets. My West preferred to sleep nude as he runs hot in his sleep and was cuddled up with me throughout the night with my body providing ample warmth.

Stuffed Animals

No stuffed animals on the sleep surface in early infancy. A special stuffed animal (or muslin) can be a great lovey, or alternate sleep cue association, that can be cuddled during the bedtime routine and then planted in the sleep garden for your little one to turn to when they wake during the night. You can set it just off the sleep surface or just out of the sleep zone during early infancy and then cuddled up with your babe as they grow.

Books

Board books that you read during the bedtime routine and then plant in the space can be yet another cue for sleep that fills your little one with all those feelings of security and love. As your child grows a more substantial collection, reading at bedtime helps to relax the body, occupy a busy mind, and trigger imagination for the dream world, all while reminding their subconscious of the secure connection you have shared.

Taste

Breasts

Nursing should be available throughout the night as needed.

Water

A cup of water they can manage can be a helpful addition for a thirsty little one around the age of 1.

Sight

Nightlight

Not all little ones need a nightlight, but the natural fear of our nocturnal predators makes bringing one into the space wise. Orange/red/yellow hues trigger sleepiness while white/blue hues trigger awakening. An on button that your little one can master at a young gives them another tool in their environment to learn to meet more of their own needs.

Calming Décor

Forgo the stimulation of bright primary colors and graphic design accents in favor of a soothing surround.

Neutrals, low contrast, softness, cleanliness, openness, and warmth all convey a cozy and peaceful sleepscape.

Clothing

Clothing is the only other thing that should be in your child's sleepscape (in the sleeping room). Clothing should be tidy and folded or hung in a dresser or closet.

Diapering

A changing pad can be on the dresser with diapers, wipes, and coconut oil (great for rashes) in the top drawer.

Sound

Sound Machine

The sound of your nearby beating heart and breathing is the song of comfort to a baby who even goes so far as to use those cues to set their own rhythms. A sound machine with sounds of the womb, nature (I recommend starting with whale sounds), calming music (60 bpm) or even white noise can help to soothe your little one through those sleep cycle transitions. Like the nightlight, an on button that your little one can easily master creates a wider path for independence.

Smell

Essential Oil

An essential oil diffuser with lavender or chamomile can add to the calm and relaxation.

Your Scent

Your scent is the most relaxing scent to your little one, so the more of your essence that is in the sleepscape, the more soothed your baby is with every inhale. Place the shirt you wore that day nearby or stuff your babe's lovey in your bra in the evening, and you will blanket the sleeping space with your intoxicating scent.

Join

Spend time connected with your little one in this restful space to extend all those feelings of security and warmth (including bonding hormones and brain chemicals) from your arms to the entire room.

Safety

A safe setup combined with the freedom and guidance your child needs to learn to interact with their environment safely is an integral part of a healthy sleepscape.

Outlets

Cover outlets in use with slide locking faceplates or plug covers for unused outlets (to prevent electrocution).

Tethers

Tether furniture like a dresser to the wall with an anchor (to prevent crushing from falling furniture).

Heavy Items

Remove heavy items from shelves that could be pulled down onto your little one (like lamps and picture frames that might be sitting on the dresser).

Bed

Remove any bed frame (except the crib in a side-car setup) and place the mattress(es) directly on the floor (to prevent injury from rolling off at a high height). You can sleep on the outer edge of the mattress while your baby sleeps between you and the wall. If you sometimes find your little one has rolled or scooted off the mattress, you can place a pool noodle under the edge of the fitted sheet and it acts as a sort of bumper.

Exploration

Allow your little one to fully and playfully explore their sleep environment so that you can guide them in interacting with the things in their space safely (as opposed to the mainstream approach of trying to block them off from everything). Instead of, "No, don't touch that," "Here's how you use that."

Safe Sleep

The goal for nighttme with your baby should be the restful harmony of you both. You should combine your intimate knowledge of your baby with information such as safe sleep guidelines to make informed choices for your baby's nights. Since you require time "off the clock" to sleep, there are hours each night when your baby is unmonitored by your attentive eye. Not to make sleep any harder for you than it already is, but this can be a risky time for your baby. Thankfully, there are some steps you can consider in setting up a sleep environment that reduce that risk. The point is not that you must implement every suggestion but that you consider making some adjustments to keep your baby as safe as possible, which will ultimately provide you with more restful sleep as well.

The Seven SIDS Risk-Lowering Steps, according to the Sears Family of Pediatricians:[17]

1. Give your baby a healthy womb environment.
2. Do not allow smoke around your baby—pre- or postnatal.
3. Put your baby to sleep on their back or side, not on their stomach.
4. Breastfeed your baby.
5. Give your baby a safe sleeping environment.
6. Avoid overheating your baby during sleep.
   This is one of my favorite tips because it is so easy to implement. Parents are often pressured to almost compulsively overheat babies. I can't tell you how many times someone told me, "Oh, he's cold; he needs a blanket," when I knew that he was perfectly content. This is one of the easiest things to adjust to make the environment a little safer with no downside. Simply apply one

less layer. Keep the room even one degree cooler. Such a simple adjustment can reduce the risk of SIDS for your baby while sleeping by preventing overheating.
7. Practice the "high-touch" style of attachment parenting.
Being physically close and emotionally responsive will help your baby to physically and psychologically thrive, meaning reduced stress hormones and increased levels of all the things that help to keep your baby safe at night.

SIDS Prevention, according to the AAP (American Academy of Pediatrics):[18]
1. Breastfeed your baby.
2. Immunize your baby.
   Reminder: These are from the AAP, not me. I've not seen any evidence-based connections between immunizations and sleep.
3. Don't use bumper pads in cribs.
   They're cute and cuddly looking, I know. Ill-advisedly, they are frequently even still included in many prepackaged crib bedding sets. Here's the bottom line: babies have suffocated in crib bumpers. No babies have died rolling into the side of the crib.
4. Put your baby to sleep on their back.
   Note: You don't have to *keep* your baby on their back through the night if they change positions of their own volition. Once Baby is able to roll on their own, they are allowed to change position at their discretion. Upon reaching this milestone, you may enjoy an increase in unassisted sleep time.

5. Provide a firm sleeping surface.
6. Keep soft objects and loose bedding out of the sleeping environment.
7. Don't smoke during pregnancy.
8. Have a separate but proximal sleeping environment.
   Baby should sleep within sensory range. Translation: you should be able to see and hear your baby all night long.
9. Offer your baby a pacifier.
   The language here is important. *Offering* your baby a pacifier can reduce the risk of SIDS. Keeping them plugged all the time comes with a whole set of other risks.
10. Avoid overheating.
11. Avoid commercial SIDS prevention devices.
    How could you not find this tip hilarious? Did you read that? Any device that is marketed as reducing the risk of SIDS actually *increases* the risk! For example, those side-sleep positioners were popular when my niece was a baby 20 years ago. They were all the rage in "reducing the risk of SIDS." The only problem: They actually increased the risk of SIDS. The AAP does not go on to explain why this phenomenon exists, though I personally suspect that the risk of SIDS increases whenever any device believed to reduce nighttime mortality risk is used, because parents then completely shut down at night instead of instinctively sleeping with "one eye open," keeping an eye on Baby's chest moving up and down, and listening for sounds of strong breathing and periodic stirring.
12. Don't use home respiratory or cardiac monitors.

13. Avoid the development of positional Plagiocephaly (Flat Head Syndrome). Babywearing (to avoid time in all those hard plastic baby containers like car seats that come out of the car, swings, bouncy seats, crib mattresses, strollers, etc.) and side-lying nursing can help tremendously as your baby is kept without firm pressure on the back of the skull and the tendons in their neck are comfortable when they sleep with their head turned to the side.

The Back to Sleep campaign has reduced the incidence of infant death from SIDS. An infant is diagnosed with SIDS when there is no found cause of death. Placing your baby to sleep on their back reduces your baby's risk of dying from SIDS because babies sleep deeper and longer when sleeping on their stomachs (the pressure is on their front just like on home base on your chest). While that sounds nice, it means that your baby will be less likely to wake for systems checks to ensure that they are still breathing and all their systems are still functioning properly. In addition to more frequent waking and lighter sleeping, another side effect of this sleep position is an increase in the risk for Flat Head Syndrome. Bed-sharing babies usually do not have this problem because they sleep with their heads turned to the side for frequent breastfeeding. So while they are sleeping on their backs, there is no pressure on the back of the skull. You can train your baby to sleep in this position by breastfeeding them while they are lying on their back and you are lying on your side next to them on your bed. You can position a pillow behind your back for additional support if necessary. Occasionally breastfeeding in this position is usually enough to encourage your baby to sleep on their back with their head turned to the side.

Altogether

Designing your little one's sleepscape around their sensory, attachment, and autonomy needs does far more in promoting better sleep than most realize. Sometimes in working with even the most challenging and heavily diagnosed sleepers, this piece is the one that was missing from their puzzle and brings the whole family tremendous peace and rest. Clear away the nursery formula you inherited and combine evidence-based information with your special expertise in your baby to create the sleepscape of your dreams.

4

SLEEP ROUTINE

Now that you know where you'll be for dreamland, how do you get there? The tone of your nights will be set by your nighttime routine; that is, the journey from the wild waves of the awake world to the calm shores of slumber. Cast off the stress of the stimulating world and walk hand in hand to the warm, safe harbor of a good night's sleep.

We don't want a schedule, which is an adult-imposed agenda based on the clock, but a routine, which is a predictable flow based on your child's needs. Your evening flow is your entry into the sleep cove and can set you all up for maximum restfulness. It is the difference between entering the night in a state of scarcity or a state of wholeness. We'll go over the nighttime routine, the bedtime routine, and then the early morning routine.

Nighttime Routine

The nighttime routine begins as dinner ends and carries you into the bed, where the bedtime routine takes over. This season of the day transitions the family from the daytime bustle to the nighttime calm. It needs to be predictable enough for your baby to depend on it and fill all your little one's remaining activity, nutritional, and emotional needs.

You want to move in one direction with geography and energy. For example, once upstairs to the quiet "bed" part of your routine, don't send your child back to the living room to clean up a mess. Keep the routine, geography, and energy moving toward sleep. If you jump off the bedtime train with your little one, you essentially have to begin the winding down process all over again.

> Living Room → Bathroom → Bedroom
> Fast and Loud → Slow and Quiet

This is often the most challenging part of the day with a baby as the evening witching hour can result in lots of crying and a spent mama. The Cry Baby chapter in the Sage Parenting book[3] has loads of help for this.

Activity: In your main living space, have a period of stimulating, rambunctious, physical play together. Little ones tend to get a burst of energy in the evening and are so often working through one motor development stage after another. They may be missing a full feeling of connection depending on the day (especially with a working parent). This activity fully exercises and meets all of these needs before shifting into the bedtime routine.

Bath: A shared bath is an ideal transition from high to low energy; while the warm water reminds your baby of the womb, you can do some massage while washing and add a couple drops of lavender or chamomile essential oil. They get loads of skin-to-skin contact and some extra pre-bedtime nursing, and it relaxes you both.

Pajamas: I preferred to go from the bath to a massage on the bed, and then my little co-sleepers slept in just a diaper while my chest kept them plenty warm. But I know most prefer pajamas, and some might not incorporate massage into the bedtime routine. If you do pcjamas after bath, here is the space for it.

Bedtime Routine

Blinds: Say goodnight to the world as you close the blinds together (they can see that it is dark outside).

Light: Guide your little one in turning off the bedroom light and turning on the night/reading light (a Himalayan salt lamp is my favorite).

Books: Guide your little one in choosing books for reading.

Loveys: Gather any alternate sleep cues like a special stuffed animal or blanket.

Sound: Guide your little one in turning on the sound machine, if you use one.

...our baby on the bed in front of you and ... from the body's core to relax you both ...eeper and longer sleep. (You can learn ... the Soothing Slumber video.[19])

Cuddle: Cuddle down together on the sleep surface so that all those feel good hormones that bloom in the bedtime routine blanket the sleep surface on which your baby will wake during the night.

Read: Read the chosen books, then place them nearby.

Nurse: Breastfeed (or offer a bottle).

Lullaby: Hum a lullaby, which engages special parts of your baby's brain while providing yet another sleep cue association that your child can engage on their own (they can hum and find the vibrations soothing).

Offer

Sleep is not something you do to a child. It is not something you impose against their will. It is something you lovingly offer. It is not banishment but a seamlessly inclusive part of your family's life. Create the optimal conditions that invite slumber. Extend an invitation to sleep. Only your baby can choose to walk through the door to dreamland. Let go of your attachment to their choice. It is not a battle wherein if your baby doesn't sleep when you command, you lose. Teach your baby to listen to their body and create a soothing sleep environment. Then go about your life.

Shift

This is one of the most important pieces to long-term healthy sleep that is restful and harmonious for parents and little ones: *shift from pouring energy into your baby, to passively being present with your baby*. Move through your bedtime routine on the sleep surface and then sleep, read your own book, or model some other relaxing behavior that you enjoy doing in the evenings while being an emotional anchor of calm, confident, peaceful love with your baby. This is a departure from mainstream parenting in that we aren't "putting" our babies to sleep. We aren't forcing something on them. We are offering and then doing what makes us happy while mothering. This simple shift is the key to offering the space for your little one to learn to fall asleep on their own without any feelings of abandonment or physiological and psychological damage from sleep training based on disconnection.

While my babies cuddled and drifted off to sleep on me, I finished up any work on my laptop (like writing this book), read a book, hung out with my husband, or watched some television. I was not trying to make them sleep. I was inviting them to sleep by providing the opportune conditions while going about doing the nighttime activities I enjoyed. You can release some of the pressure to get your baby to sleep by incorporating what you want to do at nighttime into your baby's routine. What would you be doing at nighttime if you did not have your little one? So many families with "sleep problems" come to me saying, "I try to put her to sleep at 7:30 but it takes an hour, and I dread it all day long and get so frustrated because I feel like I'm failing." How about you just go about your life and let them fall asleep when they are tired? Problem solved. Send the message that it is now nighttime, engage in activities that encourage sleep and trust that your baby will sleep when they are tired.

Duration

When it comes to the duration of your bedtime routine, you also have to think about for how long you and your partner unwind before sleep takes hold. Some people fall asleep as soon as their head hits the pillow, but that is definitely the exception. I know I like to read, cuddle, talk with my husband, maybe even watch a show together. I'm in bed relaxing for at least 2 hours before I fall asleep. Little ones need that period of unwinding just like you.

Boundary

Our family's nighttime boundary is that at nighttime we are in bed. My babies can have my cuddles, mommy milk, massage, a lullaby, books, a lovey (though they typically only attach to a lovey when they night wean) but we do not get out of bed before sunrise. They have everything they need. This consistent difference between night and day helps to establish your baby's circadian rhythm, setting their days and nights.

When your little one is in their own room, the bedroom is a good boundary. This is not to say that they cannot come to you with a need or use the bathroom. But the normal, cozy routine and expectation of where we are at night falls into the boundary.

If you are coming to this path later, your baby will learn this boundary by you gently placing them back on the bed anytime they get down. If you have always poured energy into your baby to "get" them to sleep, they may be confused and scared by the change of falling asleep on the sleep surface. Be with them while they feel their feelings and love them through it. With consistency and your calm, loving confidence, they will move through this shift quickly as they learn to fall asleep in passive connection.

Consistency

Having a bedtime routine that works for your family is so important. Children are comforted by a routine. When they know what to expect, they are more calm and cooperative. After a while with a set routine, it seems to run itself as all the moving parts, almost unconsciously with muscle memorization, go through the motions. One study showed that "those who had consistently followed the bedtime routine every night reported significantly fewer night wakings and found it easier to get their child to sleep. An added benefit was that the mothers in the bedtime routine group also felt that there had been a positive effect on their own mood."[20]

It's best to start your bedtime routine one hour before bedtime. This will lower your child's activity level and prepare their nervous system for relaxation. When it comes to the actual time of bedtime, you should do what is in the best interest of your child and what works best for your family. Every person, including young children, has a natural rhythm. You should respect your child's natural rhythm in deciding on a bedtime. Honestly, we prefer "flow." We have a couple touchstones as we flow through our evenings (like hitting the bed around 9) that provide a small amount of structure for our sleep migration, yet our sequence is consistent.

Bedtime

Common Misconception: Children need a strict bedtime. I am an advocate of teaching your children to listen to their bodies. Babies are born with an amazing mind-body connection. If nothing else, they know when they are hungry and tired, and strictly scheduling babies can disrupt this connection. This fluency can continue throughout childhood. Instead of telling your child to clean their plate, ask them to close their eyes and listen to their tummy. "Is your body telling you that you are hungry?" The same is true for sleep. As children get older, nighttime can become a power struggle between parent and child (more about compliance with authority than their own need for restorative rest). Instead, encourage children to listen to their bodies, recognize the signs of sleepiness, and respect them. Have a good nighttime routine and keep moving in the direction of bed. Enjoy a peaceful bedtime routine of connection. Cultivate a soothing sanctuary where your child is free to relax and rest in addition to sleep.

In my family, we are all happier and highly functional

at night and pretty miserable and not anywhere near as functional in the morning. When left to his own devices, my firstborn would stay up later than most and sleep in later than most (thankfully, all three of our children inherited my husband's and my night owl rhythm). My husband used to get home from work at 7:30 p.m. in our early days of parenthood. If we had put my son to bed at, say, 7:30 p.m., like a lot of parents think they "should" or are "supposed" to do, he would have had no time with his daddy, fought going to sleep, and been grumpy all morning. Instead, we listened to the needs of our child and considered what was in the best interest of our family and focused on a 9 p.m. bedtime. He functioned so well in harmony with his natural rhythm, his relationship with his daddy flourished, and we were all happier for it. You cannot change your child's natural rhythm. If you have an early morning riser—a child who truly flourishes while waking with the sun—there is no amount of maneuvering that can change this. Disharmony can exist when a parent has one natural rhythm while their child prefers the opposite schedule. If you try to bend your child to your will, you both will fail. The most you can do in this situation is prepare your environment and routine to meet both your needs as well as possible.

Sleep Crutches

It really rubs me the wrong way when sleep trainers describe breastfeeding and holding a baby as "crutches." Crutches are for people who are broken and unwell. Babies who are held and breastfed are the exact opposite, the exact way they are supposed to be: whole, complete, well, and thriving. When your nighttime routine revolves around togetherness, a crib isn't home—YOU are home. This is the exact opposite conceptualization of that offered by sleep trainers. They see you as a sleep crutch and having a bonding-based nighttime routine as a limitation. I see cribs, swaddles, and sound machines as sleep crutches. All that my babies needed to sleep was me, so we were free to do anything and be anywhere. They were not dependent on "things." This made my life easy. My babies became fully integrated into my life and our nighttime routine met all of our needs.

Habits

Some parents are concerned that if they grant their child a time of sleep dependency, they will build habits that will result in a child who is unable to sleep on their own. Prematurely forcing your baby to sleep in isolation breeds an association between sleep and feelings of abandonment. Teaching your baby that sleep is a safe and peaceful time is a much better lesson. Fostering a positive relationship between your child and sleep should be the long-term sleep goal. A child who is taught that sleep is a warm and peaceful part of the day in which the loving care to which they are accustomed is continued, and that we should look for and respect the signs of sleepiness, is contentedly willing to sleep.

Common Misconception: *If you don't put your baby to bed while they are still awake, they will never learn to fall asleep on their own.* The logic behind this is that if you put your baby to bed while they are still awake, they will learn to self-soothe. This idea came out of the big push for independence on the wave of Cry-It-Out (CIO). "In short, it is biologically, neurologically and physically impossible for a baby, toddler or even perhaps a pre-schooler to be able to 'self-soothe'. Their brains are too immature. It's like trying to teach a three-month-old baby to walk or a one-year-old to have a full-on conversation with you."[1] Babies are dependent, as Mother Nature designed. If you look at the entire lifespan of a human being, babies only need you for such a short period of time; your child could live to be 100 and might need you at night for 2 years. If you allow them to be dependent while it's appropriate, they will establish security and feel safe and confident enough to be independent for those following 98 years. *Babies learn to self-soothe by being soothed!* Developmental psychologists throughout history agree that the first task of infancy is establishing trust in caregivers and the world. Once this is firmly established they can move into establishing independence. Focusing on creating a safe and peaceful nighttime is a much better use of your efforts than fighting this period of need. Sleep will not be a power struggle against you, so your baby will respect the cues of their tired body and fall asleep independently as soon as they are ready.

Controlled Crying

That said, unlatching while your baby is drowsy but awake is one way to dissociate nursing from sleeping, if you feel the need. Some utilize this approach with crib sleeping in training a baby to fall asleep inside a crib and not on/with their person by laying the baby in the crib when drowsy but awake and attempting to soothe without picking up. Then, if the baby cries hysterically, they pick Baby up and soothe until drowsy, then lay Baby back in the crib, and repeat until the baby eventually falls asleep on the sleep surface.

This is what is referred to as "controlled crying," which can be even more harmful than CIO as the prolonged and confusing back and forth nature of your support can be quite traumatizing. The Australian Association of Infant Mental Health (AAIMH) warns: "[We are] concerned that the widely practiced technique of controlled crying is not consistent with what infants need for their optimal emotional and psychological health, and may have unintended negative consequences. . . . Crying is a signal of distress or discomfort from an infant or young child. Although controlled crying can stop children from crying, it may teach children not to seek or expect support when distressed." Most are surprised to learn that, " . . . most of the research undertaken to prove the safety and efficacy of sleep training clearly shows that, in the long term, sleep training is not effective."[1] It's interesting that, "Despite substantial investment in recent years in implementation and evaluation of behavioral interventions for infant sleep in the first 6 months, these strategies have not been shown to decrease infant crying, prevent sleep and behavioral problems in later childhood, or protect against postnatal depressions."[22] "In addition, behavioral sleep interventions risk unintended outcomes, including increased incidence of problem crying, premature cessation of breastfeeding, worsened maternal anxiety, and, if the infant is required to sleep either day or night in a room separate from the caregiver, an increased risk of Sudden Infant Death Syndrome."[1] As we are setting up sleep arrangements that allow for connection, this does not need to be a part of our nighttime parenting.

Check Out/Check In

As your child grows, if you find your presence fuels your child's wakeful energy or you are wanting to step away more during that window when the bedtime routine ends and sleep takes hold, I have developed a method I call "check out/check in." Begin by moving through your bedtime routine as usual and then one time, for a very brief period of time, check out, then immediately and consistently return. It is best if you check out to engage in a practical task that is nearby and your child can visualize you doing, for example, using the bathroom or folding the laundry in the doorway. If your child gets up to follow you, gently and calmly guide them back to bed and try again. Then slowly, over time, using their comfort level as a gauge, extend the duration of the check out time. This might look like beginning with a two-minute bathroom check out for a few days, then a five-minute check out to change over the laundry, then 10 minutes to empty the dishwasher, then 15 minutes to take a shower. ("I'm going to go get clean because I'm so dirty from today's playing. You can hear the water running and then I'll come back to our cuddle all nice and clean.") After a while, you will realize that you are no longer checking out, but checking in. I want to expressly state that without this strategy, your child will eventually fall asleep on their own with no problems. The independence will blossom naturally in its own time. This is just a gentle approach to help support your family's needs if something about that natural timeline is no longer working.

Co-Parent Support

Sometimes, particularly in that adjustment period while finding your places in the new order, co-parents (usually dads) can be unsupportive of healthy nighttime routines. This is usually expressed through criticism, seeking and pointing out perceived failures, or even withdrawal. I urge you to ask the powerful question, "What is your unmet need? What is it that you feel you need from me (or Baby) that you are not getting during our nighttime routine? How can we meet that need in ways that incorporate our new roles as co-parents?" See the Sex After Baby chapter of the Sage Parenting book[3] for more resources on successfully moving through this issue.

Early Morning Routine

Your baby's first stretch of sleep is their deepest and longest. The second part of the night, or the early morning hours, consists of lighter sleep in which your baby has a higher level of need to make up for the solitary stint of late night. Anticipate this pattern and adjust accordingly. For example, many little ones sleep on their own sleep surface for the first part of the night and enjoy shared sleep for the second half of the night.

My Journey

My nighttime routine with my babies began with a bath together followed by a massage for them and a period of time for me to unwind while they cluster fed for a couple hours. When I was ready for sleep, I laid them on their side-carred bed next to me, and they had a long stretch of sleep when we could both get some restorative rest. At some point they began to stir, and I effortlessly slid them close, settled into a good cuddle, and latched them for a few more hours of breastfeeding and dozing together. This was the picture of my harmonious nights with my babies: our perfection.

I so looked forward to my every night with a little one on my chest and boys on my shoulders. It was such a gift to end each day feeling their energy drain away with each loving stroke and leading their minds on a journey through their imaginations with great books. They peacefully breathed out their last conscious thoughts of the day and blissfully released their hold on the physical world, safe in our nest, adrift in our connection with each other. They fell asleep every night with a smile on their faces—and so did I.

As my boys have grown, the sleeping spaces have become far more permeable. We still meet in the family bed for cuddly story time around 9 (and now the books are so good!), but then the bigger boys usually migrate to their own spaces where they are free to relax in their own unique ways (often reading books or listening to audio books). Both connection and independence are always available in whatever form a child needs on any given night, but our flow is consistent and relaxing for us all.

As They Grow

Nighttime can be a stressful time in some households as exhausted parents battle children desperate for connection at the end of a long day. Once you move beyond infancy and toddlerhood it can be challenging to maintain the sense of harmony with bedtime within the mainstream lifestyle in the face of work priorities, school demands, and busy schedules; for example, a child needs at least two hours at home before bedtime to allow the elevated cortisol levels from daycare or school to fall. (I encourage you to read the Lifestyle Design chapter in the Sage Parenting book[3] or the Sage Homeschooling book[22] to consciously design your life for peace and fulfillment.) Resentments harbored from negative interactions from the day can carry over into this most special time of the 24-hour cycle. Instead of allowing bedtime to become the result of whatever is left over of everyone's patience, you can harness its potential as a sanctuary of decompression, connection, and acceptance. Ending your days in this way allows peace and love to wash away any negativity for a restful night for child and parent.

Connection

Bedtime should be a time of connection. Days can be busy; a lot of nighttime misbehavior stems from children searching for that connection—loving, focused attention. Let your children know that you are there for them, you love them, and they are important to you. This can be accomplished by incorporating some components such as mental connection, physical connection, and a send off into your bedtime routine.

Listening Time

A lot of children seem to be spilling over with things to say as their parents are tucking them into bed. Children want to be heard, and with the chaos of the world snuffed out by the nighttime routine, there is now clear space between you and them. They need you to listen and you need to hear what they have to say. Once in bed, I recommend a brief listening time—a meeting of the minds. Build into the routine 10 minutes just to listen reflectively to what your child has to say. When provided this cathartic listening time, children tend to be more accepting of sleep time, feeling like they got everything off their chests, put down all of the balls they were juggling, and emptied their racing minds.

Physical Connection

Incorporating some type of loving, physical connection will help your child to thrive. All humans need affection to survive. Bedtime is the perfect time to fill your child's love cup, raising the levels of all those feel-good hormones, which will bring more consistent and restful all-night sleep. A nightly massage is ideal as it offers a myriad of physical benefits in addition to the emotional benefits of nurturing touch. My children get to "pick a part" for massage or ask me to lightly rub their back as part of their bedtime routine. My son may choose his feet, for example, and enjoy a nice, brief foot massage. The look on his face says it all—blissful, contented relaxation. The Sage Baby class[23] or Soothing Slumber video[19] teaches a perfect set of easy-to-learn strokes that can be seamlessly adapted as your child ages. When I was young, my mom and dad would "tickle, scratch, rub" my back every night, and I would fall blissfully asleep feeling loved and safe, regardless of the frequently tumultuous state of my childhood. But this time of physical connection can look like cuddling for story time or running your fingers through your child's hair affectionately through listening time. Remember that your child's control over their body should always be respected (and empowered), so take your child's lead in what form and level of physical affection is most soothing to them.

Story Time

Story time is such a valuable component of the bedtime routine. Research shows that reading stories with your kids at bedtime fosters parent-child bonds, quickens their mastery of language, improves logic skills, and lowers stress levels.[24] One study that included storytelling in addition to story reading found that "... regular bedtime stories not only help to increase the total duration of a child's sleep, but also help them to develop intellectually and reduce bad behavior."[1] My children learned to read through our nightly story times. Even my littlest one would fall asleep on my chest as we moved through the story time phase of the nighttime routine, just listening to the sound of my voice through my chest melodically reading books. You can acquire an expansive personal library, utilize new media in the form of e-books read on the iPad or through a library style subscription app like Epic,[25] and/or check out stacks of books from your local public library, which is super fun. There are so many wonderful books out there, so many stories to send off your child's imagination into dreamland.[26]

Sleep as Punishment

Do not use sleep or bedtime as a punishment. A parent who uses sleep as a punishment ("You are now going to bed 30 minutes early!") breeds resentment and makes an enemy out of nighttime. You will wedge issues that are between you and your child in between your child and their sleep. When your child's bed is a place of punishment, they will resist going to bed. Sleep will become associated with feelings of disapproval, shame, isolation, anger, and sadness and your child will resist engaging in an activity that brings about those feelings. Reserve bedtime to be a time associated with positive feelings so your child will be free to base sleep decisions on the cues of their body's tiredness.

Altogether

Nighttime with your child can be whatever you make it. If you view it as a stressful chore, then it will be one. It is without a doubt my favorite time of the day. Using a little structure and some good strategies, nighttime is a rewarding time in which my relationship with my children grows deeper. The stress of the day is melted away by our emotional connection, and the slate is cleared for a new day brimming with potential.

5

SLEEP NEGLECT

Put Cry-It-Out to Bed

Sleep Training
Sleep is not learned.

"There *are* gentle alternatives, yet we must beware the wolf in sheep's clothing. Many methods that claim to be gentle are anything but."[1] There are a lot of sleep trainers out there who will begin by espousing the importance of sleep for your baby's health and then explain that it is your responsibility to teach (force) them to sleep. Sleep is *not* a learned behavior. A learned behavior is something we are not born knowing how to do. Babies know how to sleep just fine. Sleeping like an adult is learned—over the course of an entire childhood as the needs of your baby's brain and body mature.

Babies are capable of and content with doing the

things evolution programmed them to do: the things that are in the best interest of their health. Your baby will happily sleep on your chest where they are being protected, soothed by your heart rate, having their temperature regulated, reminded to breath from the sensations of your breathing, bonding through skin-to-skin contact, and positioned with their upper body slightly elevated to ease digestion. They will wake every couple hours to boost oxygenation and blood flow from the increased heart rate and take in the breastmilk calories needed for healthy growth and optimal development.

Oh yes, your baby can sleep just fine. Babies sleep when they are tired. They can't tell time and they selfishly know nothing of your schedule or needs. Try to look at it from your baby's perspective. Maybe you need to "learn" to accommodate their sleep schedule so that instead of being up all night (crying alone in a crib), your baby can get some sleep (in close proximity to you). If you flip the scenario on its head, it is the exact same situation! Of course, you both need to come together and compromise some to your mutual benefit so you can both get some sleep. Utilize a sleep arrangement that meets both your needs. You need sleep too in order to give your baby the best care you can. But your sleep agenda is not inherently more valid than your baby's. Come to the table with an understanding of and respect for the fact that your baby sleeps just fine, and you are asking them to change to meet your needs just as much as your baby is asking you to change to meet theirs.

"Genetics were seemingly responsible for the sleep

habits of 47% of 6-month-old babies, 58% of 30-month-old babies and 54% of 48-month-old tots. . . . The study also tells us that methods such as cry-it-out may never work for some babies because they're simply made to awaken during the night, no matter what, and deserve comfort when they do wake. In other words, ignoring a baby who is genetically designed to awaken frequently, won't help change your baby's habits."[27]

Research
Legit science, yo.

There was a study (which proved to be a cornerstone of infant sleep research) that proved that sleep training extinguishes the communication but not the physiological distress. Even after the communication is extinguished (the baby stops crying), the stress response (elevated cortisol level) is still present! Think about that and really let it sink in. This means that Baby is not "learning to self-soothe." Baby is learning not to bother asking their mother for help when they are in distress because their mother does not care for them. Baby is not suddenly no longer in distress—they have just lost trust in their parent.[28]

This is sometimes referred to as the "defeat response" by neurobiologists. When humans feel threatened, a spike of cortisol facilitates "fight or flight." Since infants can't fight or flee, they cry out for help. When that distress call is ignored, the trauma elicits the defeat response. "Babies eventually abandon their crying as the nervous system shuts down the emotional pain and the striving to reach out."[29]

Another disturbing facet of this study taught us that through CIO, mother and baby stress levels become dissociated. Normally, when Baby is distressed, Mom is distressed, and as she tends to Baby, both stress levels are lowered. It is maternal nature at its finest. But after CIO, mothers no longer experience stress along with their babies, so Mom is not as drawn to care for Baby and thereby lower Baby's stress level. Once the communication (cry) stopped, the mother's stress went away, while the baby remained in a silent physiological panic.

This prolonged flooding of the infant's brain with the stress hormone cortisol has a plethora of scientifically documented consequences on brain development and the nervous system. It results in a child either under- or over- producing cortisol when under stress. "Too much cortisol is linked to depression and fearfulness; too little to emotional detachment and aggression."[30]

"Pain responses are activated when babies are physically separated from their caregivers. This leads to the 'underdevelopment' of receptors for serotonin, oxytocin and endogenous opioids—chemicals essential for our experience of happiness. In particular, the neural pathways formed by oxytocin released in our infancy remain with us and continue to impact our adult physiology. When these pathways are compromised it makes forming healthy, future attachment relationships challenging at best."[31]

One study looking at anxiety in rats found that low maternal nurturance during infancy failed to activate the gene that builds the neural pathway for managing anxiety. These rats remained anxious when faced with new situations for their entire lives. Our mammal brains work in the same way, having a sensitive period of brain develop that requires a high level of nurturance to develop to its healthiest, happiest potential.[32]

Remember: one of the main reasons babies wake during the night is to breastfeed. So what happens when you abandon infants' nighttime feeding needs? They literally starve. The AAP even went so far as to issue an official warning against Babywise, the most popular baby training method: ". . . On Becoming Babywise, has raised concern among pediatricians because it outlines an infant feeding program that has been associated with failure to thrive (FTT), poor milk supply failure, and involuntary early weaning. A Forsyth Medical Hospital Review Committee, in Winston-Salem N.C., has listed 11 areas in which the program is inadequately supported by conventional medical practice. The Child Abuse Prevention Council of Orange County, Calif., stated its concern after physicians called them with reports of dehydration, slow growth and development, and FTT associated with the program".[33]

That "involuntary early weaning" is a common result of sleep training. You may have had a successful nursing relationship, but once the trauma of sleep training sets in, your baby enacts what is sometimes referred to as a "nursing strike"—refusing to breastfeed altogether. If you find yourself in this position, I recommend the immediate help of a lactation consultant and, obviously, to immediately cease and desist your sleep training efforts.

Even Dr. Ferber himself, who admitted to having little knowledge of infant psychology yet pioneered the CIO approach and whose name is synonymous with CIO in verb form ("Did you Ferberize your baby?"), has since had a change of heart and mind. "The doctor says he'd just as soon it went to sleep."[34]

Common Misconception: If you pick up a baby when they are crying, you are teaching them to cry. This is a gross oversimplification: you are rewarding the behavior, thereby reinforcing it. This is taken from a very basic principle of learning psychology first studied with lab rats and frequently used with dogs. Babies are not dogs. As much as you may love your pet, it is not the same. There are far more dynamics at play with a baby than a simple behavior/reward model covers. Research has shown us that the opposite is actually true. The CIO method unfolds like this: Baby communicates a need → no response → Baby cries → no response → Baby's brain and body are flooded with the stress hormone cortisol → Baby eventually gives up and learns that their communication is not effective, caregivers are not there for them, their needs may not be met, and the world is not a safe place → Baby gives up on you, surrenders to the desperation, exhaustively passes out, and stops crying. Now try this on for size: Baby communicates a need → caregiver responds sensitively (in an appropriate and timely manner) → Baby learns that communication is effective, caregivers are present and attentive, needs will be met, the world is a safe place → Baby does not need to cry.

Anecdotal Evidence

"But my friend's baby sleeps through the night and she says her baby is Einstein reincarnate and they are closer than PB&J."

The research is clear and importantly teaches us to be very respectful of our infants' nighttime needs. Yet some parents are confused about the issue of leaving a baby to cry alone at night as a means of training the baby to sleep independently (CIO or Controlled Crying, or any other sleep training method that involves not responding to Baby's cues of distress) by what's called anecdotal evidence: "I did CIO with my kids when they were babies and they are very well-rounded children who still love me."

First, it is valuable to understand that a parent who made a certain parenting choice is drawn to seeing only what validates that choice. For example: "Baby stopped crying after I left her alone screaming for three nights. This fostered independence, so I made the right choice." Of course, that is not what happened at all, but we assign meaning to experiences that bring us the most peace. Parents who used CIO will see one example of their child being connected to them ("She wanted to cuddle this morning.") and attribute it to having a very close maternal bond. Of course, "close" is relative. Does she hate you? Of course not—you're her mother. All primate offspring have a powerful and innate connection to their mothers. Does she fully trust the security of your love? I don't know.

Second, it's all relative. Think about those kids on the playground whose parents say, "We swat our kids and they are fine," as their children run around physically bullying other children. If your threshold for "fine" is "not an ax murderer," then sure, you are coming out ahead. Your standards and goals for your child's well-being are very different from the next person's. So when parents say they used CIO and their kids are awesome, that doesn't mean they are awesome objectively, it means those parents see their children as awesome.

Third, some children are incredibly resilient. Some are much less so. Some babies could survive CIO fine. Many could not. Just as some kids can walk away from serious abuse to live successful lives while many, many more do not. The problem is, you just don't know until the damage is done. It is particularly worrisome when you think about the fact that children with a high level of need (a high potential for anxiety when older) are the very group most likely to be sleep trained.

Fourth, not everyone is clear on the difference between a baby crying-in-arms versus crying-it-out. My babies sometimes cried while I held, loved, and cared for them. That does not elicit the same stress response as CIO. It is okay for a baby to communicate their feelings with you through a cry. When the message is, "I am here for you; tell me all about it," the bond is enhanced.

Fifth, I want to add that while CIO is never in the best interest of a baby directly, there are rare circumstances in which a parent is in a position where CIO is necessary to ensure the overall safety or indirect best interest of the child. If a frustrated parent is about to shake their baby, I would prefer they place the baby in a crib and walk away for a break. We also know that children with depressed mothers sleep significantly worse.[35] So while making it clear that CIO is never in the direct best interest of a baby, I wouldn't want to ban that option from existence altogether. I just advise parents that if they choose to use CIO, it needs to be because the benefit to their baby, whatever the reason, will be worth the negative effects.

Altogether

Nights with a baby will entail less sleep than your pre-baby nights. They just will. As mentioned earlier, parenting is a 24-hour job—you don't get nights off. Your baby's needs don't set with the sun. When you chose to have a baby you signed a cosmic contract to nurture this human being, a soul on loan from the universe. You cannot "grow them up" before they are physiologically capable or psychologically ready. You don't need to teach your baby to do something infants are born doing. You just need to tap into the frequency of your little one and respect who they are and where they are right now. Achieving nighttime harmony is not a gold standard destination but a journey of living in a harmonious balance of meeting your baby's nighttime needs while getting the rest you need to lovingly parent your child. So hide the clocks, resist any temptation to seize control, and allow your mindset to shift. You can paint a beautiful and restful night with your baby. Once the sun sets on this season of infancy, you will transition into more sleep independence in stride with more independence overall.

6

Sleep Interrupted

Expectations

Night waking is completely normal and healthy. Inappropriate expectations are abnormal and unhealthy. Your friend tells you her baby sleeps through the night. Your pediatrician tells you your baby doesn't need night nursing. The pressure is immense: you are told your baby is broken, you have gone astray in your parenting, and Cry-It-Out is the solution. I call bullshit. Research shows us that most healthy babies do not sleep through the night for the first couple *years* of life. The majority of sleep problems are actually expectation problems.

In fact, the modern Western preference for separate sleep while our children are young is a major cause of many sleep problems that your child could carry with them the rest of their lives. "We sleep train our children in order that they fit into our modern lives more easily;

fool ourselves into believing that it is our offspring that have 'sleep problems', rather than opening our eyes to the real problem—the disharmony between the primal needs of our young and the expectations of the modern world. Who really has the problem?"[1]

The mainstream battle to deny your baby's nighttime needs—and they are *needs*—is one in which you don't have to engage to have restful nights. Instead, focus on shifting your approach, meeting your little one's nighttime needs in ways that also bring you the rest you need.

Sleep is not a learned behavior, so release yourself from the mainstream pressure to "teach" your little one to sleep through denial and disconnection. Sleep is natural, and as with most things, the more you respect, honor, and connect with your baby and the less you control and punish, the better off you will be in both the short and long term.

Primary Causes of Night Waking

Babies wake during the night for a reason. Many of the reasons are evolutionary defense mechanisms that serve as protective factors for Baby. You may not always be able to figure out the reasons for your baby's waking but you should respect them. It is suspected that one potential cause of infant death from SIDS is not waking when the body signals that something is wrong. Your baby is not waking during the night out of a manipulative and sadistic plot to destroy your life and break down your sanity. There are some common reasons for night waking and some preventative measures you can take to set your child up for success, maximizing the amount of sleep that is safe and healthy for *your* baby.

Circadian Rhythm

So what's wrong with these adorable little poop machines? Why aren't they born sleeping at night? They are not born with a set circadian rhythm, or synced into the sleep/awake cycles cued by the sun. The best and fastest way to set your baby's internal sleep clock (the circadian rhythm can be established between 2 and 4 months old)[36, 37] is to keep your day and night cues consistent. During the day, the blinds are open, even and especially during naps, voices are standard volume, and Baby is worn in the pouch[38] so they are safely exposed to movement, interaction, and gentle stimulation. The sun (indirect sunlight) is your most valuable asset because we are hardwired to sync with the day/night rhythms cued by the sun (soaking up that vitamin D). During the night, blinds are closed, lights are low, movement is slow and rhythmic, voices are low and calm, and stimulation limited. The biology behind breastfeeding makes night nursing a huge asset in this effort as well. Breastmilk production actually increases at nighttime[40] (thanks to nightly piqued Prolactin levels—the milk-producing hormone) to facilitate night nursing because breastmilk that is produced at night actually contains melatonin,[39] a sleep-inducing hormone that infants do not produce on their own, as well as a sleep-inducing amino acid called tryptophan.[40]

Bonding

A baby is born with a couple of pressing tasks. The first is to sucker grown-ups into a euphoric state of love assuring they will meet your needs (attachment). The process of attachment (primary emotional, psychological, and social developmental task at birth)[41] is so important that it cannot take half the day off (12–20 hours is the amount of sleep a newborn needs). One of the very common reasons for waking during the night involves hormone levels and brain chemicals. This is such a valuable task to understand because it is so common, almost impossible for parents to detect, and one for which there is much you can do to help. Within our brains we all have the feel-good chemical hormones serotorin, dopamine, and oxytocin. These hormone levels are raised by bonding interactions such as touch, breastfeeding, closeness, etc. and slowly lower when not being touched. There is a natural balance of these feel-good hormones with stress hormones such as cortisol. Cortisol is produced when a baby is alone, crying, hungry, etc. Long-term studies on cortisol and infant brain development tell us that babies with higher levels of cortisol have significant negatively impacted brain development resulting in a plethora of negative outcomes such as lower IQ and emotional regulation as well as depression and anxiety in adulthood.[42-60] When the feel-good chemical hormones dip below a certain level, the baby's brain emerges from the sleep cycle and alerts the body that the baby is not safely being cared for. For infants, safety is instinctually defined by how directly invested their caregiver is at every moment, because for an infant, neglect can be the difference between life and death. They wake, reengage their caregiver, and demand attachment-promoting behaviors that simultaneously reinvest that caregiver and raise the levels of all those feel-good hormone chemicals in their brains.

Understanding this cause of night waking from within the appropriate context shows that this reason for waking should be respected. Luckily there are many strategies for raising those feel-good hormone chemical levels, maximizing the amount of time Baby can sleep before they need a love refill. Infant massage is a particularly effective strategy because it is a supercharging attachment-promoting behavior. During infant massage, you are lovingly stroking your baby's entire body and making eye contact. Baby can feel your breath, hear your heartbeat, smell your essence; you are relaxing both yourself and your baby, soothing any discomforts from the day and sending them off to slumber with peak feel-good hormone levels. Watching the Soothing Slumber video is a nice way to learn all the baby massage strokes that are ideal for nighttime.[19] Warm baths with baby are also an effective strategy. Tons of skin-to-skin contact, milk access, gentle touch, and warm water reminiscent of the womb are all powerful feel-good hormone chemical boosters. You can even combine the two, employing infant massage strokes as you wash your baby with their soap. The easiest strategy for keeping those levels up and preventing waking is to put your baby to sleep near you. When they can smell you (one study found that a newborn could identify their mother in a lineup by smell alone[28]), feel your breath, hear your heartbeat, see you, and/or touch you, their chemical hormone levels are being fed while you are sleeping. It doesn't get much better or easier than passive nurturing, and this arrangement has the added benefit of more restful sleep for Mom.

Hunger

Breastfeeding is, of course, one of the most potent strategies, and in addition to the attachment-promoting benefit, fills their bellies and increases saliva production, which aids in nighttime digestion and brain development. Cluster feeding (where baby nurses on and off for a stretch of a few hours) is something babies do naturally that should be encouraged, as it provides parents with that valuable stretch of non-breastfeeding time that inevitably follows. This leads us to Baby's second task: gain weight. Even gaining weight (a primary physical developmental task at birth) is tied to attachment. To really thrive and put on those healthy rolls, a newborn needs to eat every 2-4 (max) hours (sometimes it looks like every 15 minutes, other times every 4 hours). This is because babies have tiny stomachs; they can only hold and digest a few ounces as newborns. So you fill them to the brim, and then a couple of hours later they are again on empty, ready for more (breastmilk takes about an hour and a half to digest). Stretching the time between feedings doesn't expand the size of your baby's stomach; it just forces your baby to sit longer in a state of hunger. Needing to eat is not a behavioral issue; it is a physical one. It's also worth noting that feeding your baby formula or solid foods prior to 6 months of age does *not* improve sleep (and leads to a whole slew of other problems like increased risk of asthma, allergies, and digestive problems).[61, 62, 63] The need for night nursing is legitimate and valid. As much as your baby loves you and wants you to be rested, they cannot change their capacity to digest. As they grow, their stomach grows, and so will the time between feedings. Feeding on cue all day and feeding Baby well their last feeding of the evening can stack all the cards in your favor.

Another great tip is to feed your baby again when you are ready to go to sleep. Babies usually have one long stretch of sleep during the night (their first sleep cycle), so feeding your baby when you are ready to go to sleep can help align their sleep cycle with yours. For example, if your baby falls asleep at 8 p.m., you are ready to go to sleep at 10 p.m., and your baby's first sleep cycle lasts four hours followed by a feeding every hour thereafter, your baby will be up at midnight, giving you only two hours of sleep. If you give your baby a twilight feeding at 10 (you don't need to fully wake them, and usually an expressed drop of milk is enough to prompt sucking), your baby can sleep until 2, giving you four full hours of sleep. This technique does not settle perfectly with every little one, as every baby is unique, and can actually disrupt extended sleep cycles and cue feeding across the board. But it is a good tool to have in your parenting toolbox to try; allow your babe to show you if it works well for them. You should also consider sleeping close to Baby. In addition to being the safest sleep arrangement, sleeping near Baby makes nighttime feedings easier. I can't tell you how often my babies breastfed during the night. Since they slept next to me, I needed only open my nursing bra when I sensed their rooting and we could both doze together.

As your little one does grow into an expanded diet, know that artificial coloring (especially red and yellow), caffeine, and monosodium glutamate are consistently linked to sleep problems in children. Dairy allergies, so common nowadays, are typically outgrown by about 5, so prior to that, keep an eye on how diary affects your specific child's digestive health and sleep. On the flip side, research shows that omega-3 supplements[64], tryptophan, and a small meal half an hour before bed can improve children's sleep.

Sleep Cycle Transitions

Babies have shorter sleep cycles and can rouse during the transition from one sleep cycle to the next (between active and quiet sleep states), about every 40 minutes. The duration of your little one's sleep cycles will extend as they grow and their brain matures slowly over time.

These shorter sleep cycles are believed to be a protective mechanism to wake up their systems and make sure they keep firing (breathing, pumping, digesting, etc.). This is an especially protective mechanism against SIDS. This is where it is important to emphasize "restful nighttime" over "sleeping through the night." You would rather have a baby whose brain is sensitive than had a baby whose brain wasn't sensitive enough.

Swaddling can be helpful during these transitions, particularly if your baby has a sensitive startle reflex, giving your infant the sense of being securely held like in the womb or your arms. For some families, swaddling is a savior that brings longer stretches of sleep and less crying, but I caution parents that this is really a soothing technique for a *newborn* (not beyond 2-4 months or once your baby can roll) as a tight swaddle can contribute to hip dysplasia, delayed rolling, missed breastfeeding cues, and Flat Head Syndrome. A baby should also never be swaddled while bed-sharing. While I didn't swaddle any of my babies, if you do find that swaddling helps your little one, I would recommend a swaddler that keeps your baby's hands up by their mouth and is loose around the lower body such that they can get in the natural frog position with their legs. White noise (waves, whales, womb, etc.) can also be helpful as little ones begin to stir. Belly to back is another great technique to have in your parenting toolbox. If your baby is waking or wakes during the transition from you to the sleeping surface, you can lay them on their belly while you are there watching. Then, after your baby has settled in and fallen into that next sleep state, you can gently roll them to their back.

Development

As babies move through developmental stages, they experience phases with high levels of nighttime need. This is not regression but progression, as new awarenesses, understandings, and skills are expressed through sleep needs.

The second day after birth is typically characterized by 24 hours of crying followed by a newborn period of lots of sleep. After that, the 4- (awareness of self as separate from mother) and 9- (separation anxiety) month leaps tend to be the most significant, followed by a spike of nighttime need around 18 months.

> "My baby was sleeping almost through the night and now he is waking every hour!"

> "You didn't break your baby. It is normal and healthy, this stage will pass, and we can shift to help you all get more rest while meeting these new needs."

You may find yourself months into a consistent nighttime routine that includes hours of uninterrupted sleeping bliss and then, all of a sudden, your little one is awake for two hours at 2:00 a.m. Do not be alarmed—you did not break your baby. It is perfectly normal for babies to change their nightlife during developmental or physical growth spurts or changes in family life. For example, if your little adventurer is right on the cusp of crawling, they may wake every night for a couple of weeks to spend an hour working on this skill. When they are mastering a new skill or exploring a new understanding, they tend to devote all of their resources (time, energy, attention) to it—and nighttime is no exception. Teething, a new level of understanding regarding strangers, and hunger brought on by a growth spurt are all examples of developmental milestones that may result in a disruption of your nighttime routine. Mom going back to work is a common culprit of nighttime unrest. If your little one can't bond with you during the day, they will adapt and try to meet those bonding needs at night (even going so far as to sleep all day with the substitute caregiver to enjoy more of their nights with you). "Mommy is sleeping, but we can cuddle here *together* while we sleep." Trust in your baby. If your baby needs some extra reassurance that you are present and keeping them safe at night, give it to them. If your baby needs to spend an hour working out at the bed gym, let them. Keep nighttime as "night" time but trust that your baby is trying to meet a need, even if you don't know what that need is. If you meet your baby's needs, they will move through the phase and come out on the other side a happy little sleeper once again.

Restricted Airway

Another cause of night waking, especially if ill, is a restricted airway. Babies are not born with fully formed sinuses. They are born with a cluster of predestined cells that are not even detectable by x-ray. The sinuses are the honeycomb structures that process and store mucus. Even with normal, healthy amounts of mucus, but especially if congested, babies struggle to breath, especially since they can only breath through their nose. If they are congested or any kind of airway blockage occurs, they lack the ability to manually alternate between nasal and oral breathing (which we are able to coordinate by maneuvering the back of our tongues), so they wake. This is glorious evolution, working its magic as a protective force to keep your baby alive. If the oxygen levels in their brain dip too low, the alert is sounded and they wake, once again, frequently crying to rapidly re-oxygenate. Babies also frequently awake with flailing arms when this particular alert is sounded, attempting to remove any external blockage of their airways. Infant massage over the face and chest, a warm bath, breastmilk, and incline (roll up a blanket and place it under the head of your baby's sleeping surface if congested) can all help to stave off the mucus bug.

Bad Dreams

Nightmares can occur during the REM sleep state and are common beginning at age 2 and peaking between 3 and 6. These nightmares usually occur toward the end of the night and are usually remembered. The causes of many nightmares can be worked out through a practical lens and resolved by making some life changes (which is almost always easier said than done, but possible). Often nightmares are a reflection of a child's permeable understanding of fantasy and reality. The solution lies in meeting the child there in that space, accepting the fears as they are for the child instead of rationally arguing against them through your adult lens. After all, many parents talk of things like tooth fairies then balk at trolls under the bed. You can read more about externalizing and personifying to resolve fears and anxieties in the Collaboration chapter of the Sage Parenting book.[3]

Night terrors are far less common and different from nightmares in that they usually occur during the first half of the night and children typically have no memory of them upon waking. A child experiencing a night terror might seem awake yet be difficult to rouse. One study with promising results shows that logging the night terror times and waking your child about 15 minutes prior extinguishes them.[1]

Bed-Wetting

Allow your children to sleep in a diaper for as long as they need. Not waking from a full bladder is normal right up to the age of about 7.[65] Read more on this in the Tarzan Pees chapter of the Sage Parenting book.[3]

Common Misconception: *Babies should sleep through the night at X months old. Babies should sleep X number of hours in a 24-hour period. Babies will sleep more or less at X months old.* If there is one thing that meta-analyses of infant sleep studies have taught us, it is that there is no objective normal for healthy infant sleep. Healthy infants are not sleeping through the night at X months of age. Period. If your pediatrician hands you a chart with ages and hours of sleep—toss it. If someone gives you a book that promises to get your baby sleeping through the night—chuck it. Your baby is unique, with their own nighttime needs that are perfectly tailored to help them thrive. More on this in the Day Sleep chapter.

While always being able to meet all the needs of your baby is ideal, parents are human beings. We need sleep. If the goal is to be the best parent you can be, then sleep for you is going to need to be in that equation. It is hard to balance the needs of your baby with your needs. This will be a balance you will work on daily for the rest of your life. Especially if you have a high needs baby, you have to give yourself permission to get the fuel you need to keep taking good care of that baby. Sometimes this might mean calling Daddy up from the batter's box (giving Daddy and Baby time to establish their connection is good for both Daddy and Baby), giving a trusted family member a shift, or leaving your baby on their sleep surface. In some families, everyone just sleeps better when their baby is in their own space, and that is perfectly okay. Doing what's best for your baby and your family is the moral of this story. Sometimes doing what's best for you is what's best for Baby in the long run.

Altogether

All of the work we have done in consciously cultivating our sleep garden will help to nurture you and your little one and allow for growth, meeting needs in ways that also grants you rest and allows for maturation in your little one. An evening routine and sleep arrangement that incorporates comfortable connection sends those bonding chemicals and hormones as high as they can go entering sleep and allows you to maintain them while sleeping yourself. This includes nursing while resting, while the nighttime boundary provides the cozy consistency that keeps you on the path. In our bedtime routine we are guiding our little ones in doing as much as they can *with* us instead of doing everything for them. This creates a path for independence as they wake during the night and have learned to utilize all these sleep cues in their environment. We have planted a sleep garden around our babies that they can grow into, meeting more of their own nighttime needs while simultaneously allowing for the connection that nurtures that growth and spurs that independence. When your baby wakes at night, consider all of the potential causes for night waking and use them to guide your attempt to meet their needs, keeping in mind that research tells us that most children won't sleep through the night until 2 and even then 55% are still waking regularly.[66]

7

SLEEP WEANING

Many breastfed toddlers reach a point when they figure out that during the day, they do not want to stop being active and having fun to breastfeed. Walking and eating new solid foods are novel skills they are just too excited about to take a break, be still, and nurse. They want to spend the whole day walking, playing, and chowing down on solid food. But they are not yet ready to wean; they still crave the nutrition from breastmilk and the bonding time from breastfeeding. Your toddler is so smart that they may realize that nighttime is boring and the perfect time to make up all that breastfeeding they have cut out of the day.

The long process of your child growing and maturing into their independence is one that they should lead. This should be extended to all aspects of parenting, including breastfeeding. However, I also understand that some people, under certain circumstances, must wean their little one at nighttime in order to get the sleep they need to be a good parent to that child. If you feel that this is the right choice for you and your baby, I can offer you a strategy for night weaning that maintains the dignity, respect, empathy, and compassion with which you parent. This strategy contains no CIO and does not deny your child you, your comfort, your contact, or your love.

Until your little one is old enough to understand what "night-night" means, they are too young for nighttime weaning. Your baby should certainly be at least 12 months old, older if you feel they don't yet have a firm grasp on this concept. I also want to be clear that this is not a strategy for weaning from breastfeeding in general or an implication, in any way, that babies should be night weaning at 12 months old. If you are happily and functionally night nursing your sweet babe, then embrace it and treasure the time, as it won't last forever, and you will look back on this precious time fondly.

The first step is to introduce your child to the concept of things going night-night. Take some time to begin pointing out all of the things and people around you going night-night like the sun, Daddy, the family pet, etc. Allow this concept to really sink in for a couple weeks. Play this concept out with your child, as play is the learning language of all children. Role-play, use toys, read books, explore nature after dark and your child will understand this concept through positive, fun, educational interaction.

You want to begin your nighttime with a nighttime routine that will help your baby to unwind, calm down, and relax while filling their love cup. I suggest something like saying goodnight to the sun and hello to the moon and stars, followed by bath, book (Nursies When the Sun Shines[66] is the perfect companion for my night weaning method), massage, and breastfeeding, as was previously discussed. Infant massage is really the perfect thing to include in your nighttime routine because, in addition to research showing that your baby can sleep longer after a massage, it addresses/prevents a lot of the causes of night waking. You can pick up the Soothing Slumber[19] video to learn this valuable addition to what you can offer your child in easing this transition. A nighttime routine rooted in connection is imperative for this process.

As you begin this transition, by pointing out that at night the world is sleeping and by setting up a good nighttime routine, also begin to build a sleep cue association. As you breastfeed your little one to sleep, introduce another cue for sleep alongside nursing. For example, softly sing a specific lullaby as you breastfeed them to sleep each night. Perhaps your little one responds well to running your fingers through their hair. Choose something to pair with nursing to sleep so that your child begins to associate all those warm, safe feelings elicited from breastfeeding with your new or additional sleep cue. Then, once the nighttime nursing is gradually removed, you have other comfort options that will be familiar and soothing.

Some children have transitional objects like a teddy bear or a baby blanket. My Sky had his "silky B." He needed only walk across it as it lay on the floor and he would collapse into a blissful, cuddly heap. My Bay never had one ... until he naturally weaned. It is common for children who have used their Mommy Milk as their primary comfort sanctuary (as well they should) to substitute with a comforting object. For Bay, who was infatuated with Peter Pan, his Peter Pan stuffed guy became his new nighttime best friend. As you are pushing this transition before it naturally evolves on its own, it can be helpful to provide options for potential transitional objects that your little one could gravitate toward as you move through the transition. So as you move through your nighttime routine, add a little company in the form of a few of their favorite soft lovies.

After you have laid the groundwork with the initial phases of the transition, it is time to set a time window when "milk is night-night." You want to tell your little one during the breastfeeding portion of their nighttime routine that just like sun goes night-night and "Baby" (insert child's name) is going night-night and Mommy is going night-night, "milk" is going to go night-night. Substitute the word "milk" with whatever word you use for breastfeeding. Set aside a brief window of time to start with when the "milk" will be night-night. "Milk" can wake up at sunrise. Since little ones can't tell time, the sun is the perfect indicator for them. For example, if you begin with a window of 4-6 a.m., you breastfeed them each time they wake until 4 a.m. At the last feeding before 4 a.m. you tell your child, "Okay, milk is going night-night. Night-night milk." When the sun wakes up, the milk wakes up. Then if they wake to breastfeed during the 4-6 a.m. window, remind them,

"Milk is night-night. When the sun wakes up, the milk wakes up." For many a better window is the first stretch of sleep, as they naturally sleep longer during the first portion of the night. In this case, milkies might be night night if and when Baby wakes before midnight.

During this time, your baby will probably be upset, and you are free to follow your maternal instincts and comfort, hold, cuddle, and love your baby. Your baby is never denied access to the caregivers who love them. Be sure to wear clothing that securely covers your breasts. I know my nursing ninjas could locate, retrieve, and latch a nipple before I even knew what hit me. Keep your breasts out of sight and locked down during this window. Sleeping topless would be like cuddling a cake while you try to kick carbs. Stick with your nighttime boundaries (keep the lights low, stay in your bedroom, etc.), which can provide familiar comfort, offer all those sleep associations and transitional objects you have been building up, and most of all, be a calm, loving, empathetic presence. Be the state you want to see in your baby, and communicate a compassionate confidence. If you trust that your little one will be okay, they will believe it, and they will.

Once your baby becomes relatively comfortable with the brief window, you can then expand that window as you desire. Move to 3-6 a.m., then 2-6 a.m., then 1-6 a.m., etc. I advise parents to ultimately land on the hours that the parent sleeps. For example, if you go to sleep at midnight, the "milk" can be night-night from midnight until sunrise. If you say "milk is night-night" and then they cry and you give them milk, it will be a much longer process with more stress and lots of tears. It is important to be consistent; that is why I advise beginning with only a very brief window of time and expanding from there.

Sleep is one of those things that you have to accept will be different when you make the decision to have a baby. If, after years of meeting your baby's nighttime needs, you feel your child is ready to transition away from nighttime as mealtime, this gentle strategy can facilitate that transition in a way that is loving and comforting and does not rely on isolation or ignoring any of your baby's cues. Using a strategy that allows you to be there and responding sensitively to any distress your baby has during this transition will extend the foundation of trust you have worked so hard to build and provide you both with more sleep.

8

Day Sleep

I stay close, knowing that based on his natural rhythm, we could be nearing a period of dormancy. He slows down. He lingers closer. Then he takes my hand and politely asks, "Mommy, sit couch, mup (mommy milk)?" We snuggle down. He nurses and leaves the conscious world swirling around him for the secure and peaceful rest of a nap.

And now I get to pull over my laptop, while my Squishy cuddles next to me, and write this piece on naps, which have to be one of the most grossly misunderstood and over-controlled aspects of parenting. I would like you to gather up every physical handout, digital file, and piece of advice you have received detailing when, how, and for how long your child should be napping, and *shred them*. Live a life you love and let sleep happen. Now let's go over the duration and location of naps as well as how awake time can enhance day sleep.

How Much

Research

There is no evidence-based amount of sleep that is healthy for a baby. Really take that in. The conclusions from the most valid and reliable meta studies on infant sleep have shown us that the variability of sleep needs from one baby to the next preclude any meaningful averages. One study puts the range between 11 and 17 hours in a 24-hour period.[68] "According to a systematic review of 22 studies on <u>normal</u> infant sleep at 2 months of age, babies' total sleep over 24 hours ranged from 9.3 to 20 hours. Yeah, it's that variable."[69] *Every little one is different.* "Much of what has been circulated in the parenting world on child sleep seems to be founded on parental convenience, rather than biology or science, and it's about time that changed."[1] The moral of this story is to take your cues from and trust your little one. Reject any pressure from outside sources and honor your individual child's needs.

Research tells us that allowing your child to sleep when they are tired is in their best interest (allowing/offering naps is good for health). What that actually looks like for your baby will be vastly different than what that looks like for your friend's kid. Your child has their own natural rhythms that, when respected, create harmony and, when disrespected, create conflict. Observe your child with a keen awareness of their cues. When do they naturally get tired? When are they their most engaged? When do they naturally rise, seeming rested? There are no absolutes in the world of naptime for children. Some thrive with short, frequent dozing on your chest while others benefit from complete, hours-long shutdowns, even into the preschool years. Honor whatever your little one shows you will help them to be their best self.

Routine

While honoring your child's natural rhythm, you will find that you fall nto a comfortable routine. A routine is a predictable sequence of events, which occur during roughly the same parts of the day, based on your child's natural rhythm. A schedule is a strict set of activities, based on the parent's agenda, that revolves around the clock. *Aim for routine.* It provides the predictability that gives children comfort and allows you to set up your life while incorporating respect for your child and the flexibility necessary to honor your child's ever-changing needs.

Flex Sleep Time

The sleep needs of your baby will change right alongside their blossoming development and maturity. *Naptime is the perfect flex sleep time.* You have a direct stake in the consistency of your child's nighttime sleep (if they are awake, so are you), but allow daytime sleep to serve as the point of expression for all those changing needs. For example, while on the verge of mastering a new level of talking, babies will frequently skip naps in favor of logging extra hours honing this new conversational skill. Perfect. While sick, babies will frequently need more naps. Perfect. Trust that they are following their brain's and body's cues and their needs will be met. Support that brain-body connection by encouraging your little one to sleep when tired, not based on a clock or authority figure's command.

Offer

Just like with food, *your job is to offer sleep, not to make them sleep. So* many parenting problems are manufactured completely from parents attempting to do what they think they are supposed to do instead of simply trusting their baby. The commonly used phrase "put them down" has always rubbed me the wrong way. It feels disrespectful. Your baby is not a toy to be shoved back on a shelf at your convenience. Most importantly, it betrays a fundamental flaw in the mainstream approach to sleep. It is not something you do to a child. It is not something you impose against their will. It is something you lovingly offer. It is not banishment but a seamlessly inclusive part of your family's day. Make this philosophical switch and you will have children who welcome sleep throughout their entire childhoods.

Natural Consequences

The most common fear I have found that holds parents back from honoring their child's sleep needs is the fear of having a cranky child. Really? You're going to spend years engaging in a battle over sleep, which overtakes your day and sanity, which you will never win (because ultimately you cannot make someone sleep), because your kid might get cranky? *Grant them permission to experience the natural consequences of life, even the ones that don't include a smile.* Your little one is not going to be happy 100% of the time. That is not a reflection of a failure on your part. That is a reflection being alive. Sometimes I get cranky. You know what helps me: understanding, patience, and extra hugs.

Pressure

If you find yourself in a position where you feel you need your child's naptime (for your to-do list and/or your sanity), you have gone astray. Do not build the tower of your day upon the block of your child's nap. *That is a lot of pressure to place on your baby.* You are holding them responsible for the success or failure of your day, and that is not fair. Construct your day around what you can accomplish with your child in tow. Take responsibility for your own state of mind and incorporate whatever self-care you require to be your best self. If they take a nap—great. If they don't sleep right now—that's okay too.

Where?

The best place for your little one to nap will vary depending on your lifestyle.

On You

Common Misconception: "Good" babies nap independently. Fact: "Over 65% of infants nap in-arms nearly everyday."[70]

If you are going about living a full life that fosters the potential and magnifies the joy in you and all your children, you are probably not sitting alone in a silent, dark house with a crib in a nursery for hour upon hour every day. If you are committed to the path of pushing premature independence (adult sleep patterns and arrangements) on your baby, you may find yourself depressingly isolated. If your baby takes two 2-hour naps a day (let's say, 10-12 and 2-4), and you are shackled to artificial containers for all that time, you can become imprisoned in your own home.

Contrary to what sleep trainers warn, attachment-based sleep is not a crutch. All the required stationary tools for disconnection are crutches.
My babies can sleep anywhere, anytime, because all they need is their loving caregiver. Today's scenario I described at the beginning of the chapter frequently plays out in the form of "Mommy, pouch (babywearing carrier), mup?" We are free to go anywhere and do anything, taking advantage of all the world has to offer. This becomes vital when you have more than one child as, for example, your elder child's class does not care if your baby would like to nap. It's pick-up time and you have to be there. Once you are in the position of having to balance the needs of multiple children, you may very well find yourself here anyway. So live your life and just let sleep happen.

A babywearing pouch (wrap or carrier) is key in living a lifestyle that fulfills you and meets your baby's needs. Whether grocery shopping, working, or playing, your little one can nurse and nap right there in their home base whenever tired (you can learn more about how to master babywearing in the Babywearing chapter of the Sage Parenting book).[3]

The breastfeeding on cue, skin-to-skin contact, holding,

face time, etc. of daytime connection, including during naps, promotes *more and better* nighttime sleep. Content, secure, and loved become the default settings of your child's core and that grants you more peaceful nights.

In Bed

If the bulk of your days are spent at home and you would rather your baby napped on the sleep surface, you always have that option. You would simply engage the bedtime routine, with Baby falling asleep on the sleep surface, and then you would be free to leave the room. The only difference from bedtime would be that the blinds should always be open during the day, exposing your little one to indirect sunlight to help establish that circadian rhythm. The upside to napping in bed would be that you could run around the house baby-free. The downside would be that your baby would have a harder time falling asleep when out of the house, and unless you are remaining in the bedroom with your baby for the whole nap, it also increases the risk of daytime SIDS. ("75% of the daytime SIDS deaths occurred while babies were alone in a room."[1])

As your baby gradually transitions into a child, you may find yourself in a nice, long period where your little one no longer needs a true nap (I won't use the word resists, as that implies attempted force) but still benefits greatly from the calm, centering break naptime used to provide. *For this I recommend changing "naptime" to "rest time" or "quiet time."* Set some ground rules that you think would most facilitate the experience your child needs. For example, "It seems to me that your body is telling you that you don't need sleep right now. I also see that you have a lot of frustration, and it seems to me that your coping cup is full. So we are going to have rest time so that all that frustration can run right out of your cup while you have some time to relax." This will look different for every child; maybe it's a quiet time on the bed with stuffed animals and books. "You don't have to sleep, but you do have to stay in this quiet space with calm words and a calm body." For my little one, I simply invite him to cuddle with me and read some books or go for a walk outside in the pouch. It provides the quiet, centering moment he needs.

Awake Time

One key piece to nap time (and nighttime sleep) is actually your awake time. Your little one needs periods of time to exercise their needs (from fun energy to calm stillness to hypnotic connection). All this can be done while out and about with a bit of mindfulness and a pouch (babywearing carrier). Be sure you are incorporating ample skin-to-skin and face-to-face time while awake (or they will need to seek it while tired).

- Time Outside: at least 20 minutes each day
- Vigorous, High-Contact Play: like patty cake for a very young one or gentle, playful wrestling for an older baby
- Feeding: on cue breastfeeding and complimentary food after 6 months
- Relaxed Play: like sitting on the floor with some

fine motor toys
- Bonding Time: at least half an hour of focused time together daily, which can incorporate any of these activities
- Bedroom Time: allow your child to fully explore and interact with their sleep environment while awake so that all those curiosities and drives are satisfied before sleepiness sets in.
- Walking: the last step, for an intense baby especially, is to hold them in your arms and walk together. This can be just around your house while you sing a lullaby for about 10 minutes.

Live your life. Allow them to sleep when they are tired. Voila.

THE NEXT STEP

Welcome to the Sage Parenting family!

Coaching

You've read the guidebook for walking the Sage Sleep path; it's a journey that is endlessly fulfilling and rarely perfect. That's why I offer one-on-one coaching. This guidebook can take you so far, but sometimes you just need a personalized guide in your pocket (that's me—it's cozier in here than you might think). Every little one is unique, so sometimes a general theme won't fit without the customized piece to translate it into your child's natural language. I'm here. I see you. I can help, with small shifts that yield huge results. And because you are now in the club, you get to enjoy 10% off your first coaching package with the code LOYALSAGE.

Books

Sleep is one trail on the Sage Parenting path. Breastfeeding, homeschooling and parenting are important trails on the Sage Parenting path. So important, in fact, that they have their own guidebooks. Sage Sleep is book one in a four-part series. Walk deeper down the path with:

Sage Parenting: Honored and Connected
Sage Breastfeeding: Nourished and Connected
Sage Homeschooling: Wise and Connected

REFERENCES

1. The Gentle Sleep Book: https://gentlesleepbook.com
2. The Attachment Parenting Book: https://www.amazon.com/Attachment-Parenting-Book-Commonsense-Understanding-ebook/dp/B000Q67H4A/ref=sr_1_1?s=digital-text&ie=UTF8&qid=1463452957&sr=1-1&keywords=the+attachment+parenting+book
3. Sage Parenting Book: http://www.sageparenting.com/sage-parenting-book/
4. Dr. James McKenna: http://cosleeping.nd.edu/mckenna-biography/
5. Dr. Jay Gordon: http://drjaygordon.com
6. Sears Family of Pediatricians: http://www.askdrsears.com
7. Attachment Parenting International: http://www.attachmentparenting.org
8. Mothering: http://www.mothering.com
9. Peaceful Parenting: http://www.drmomma.org
10. Learning to Trust Our Intuition: http://pathwaystofamilywellness.org/Parenting/learning-to-trust-our-intuition.html
11. Cosleeping is Twice as Safe by Tina Kimmel: http://www.mothering.com/community/a/cosleeping-is-twice-as-safe
12. The Changing Concept of Sudden Infant Death Syndrome by the American Academy of Pediatrics: http://pediatrics.aappublications.org/content/116/5/1245.full

13. Outcome correlates of parent-child bedhsaring: an eighteen-year longitudinal study: http://www.ncbi.nlm.nih.gov/pubmed/12177571
14. Child behavioural problems and body size among 2-6 year old children predisposed to overweight. Results from the "healthy start study': http://www.ncbi.nlm.nih.gov/pubmed/24250821
15. A Longitudinal Study of Bed Sharing and Sleep Problems Among Swiss Children in the First 10 Years of Life: http://pediatrics.aappublications.org/content/115/Supplement_1/233
16. New Research: Does Solitary Sleep Increase the Risk for Insecure Attachment?: http://evolutionaryparenting.com/new-research-solitary-sleep-insecure-attachment/
17. 7 Steps to Reduce the Risk of the Risk of SIDS: http://www.askdrsears.com/topics/sleep-problems/sids/7-steps-reduce-risk-sids
18. The Changing Concept of Sudden Infant Death Syndrome by the American Academy of Pediatrics: http://pediatrics.aappublications.org/content/116/5/1245.full
19. Soothing Slumber Video: http://www.sageparenting.com/soothing-slumber-video/
20. A nightly bedtime routine: impact on sleep in young children and maternal mood: http://www.ncbi.nlm.nih.gov/pmc/articles/PMC2675894/
21. Behavioral sleep interventions in the first six months of life do not improve outcomes for

mothers or infants: a systematic review: http://www.ncbi.nlm.nih.gov/pubmed/24042081
22. Sage Homeschooling: http://www.sageparenting.com/sage-homeschooling-book/
23. Sage Baby Class: http://www.sageparenting.com/sage-baby-class/
24. The Brainy Benefits of Bedtime Stories by Patti Jones: http://www.parents.com/fun/entertainment/books/the-brainy-benefits-of-bedtime-stories/
25. Epic: https://www.getepic.com
26. Our Children's Book Favorites: http://www.sageparenting.com/childrens-book-favorites/
27. Sleep Training Debunked: Study Finds Genetics Play a Large Role in Baby's Sleep Habits: http://www.inhabitots.com/sleep-training-debunked-study-finds-genetics-play-a-large-role-in-babys-sleep-habits/
28. Babies left to cry 'feel stressed,' research finds: http://www.telegraph.co.uk/news/health/children/9286683/Babies-left-to-cry-feel-stressed-research-finds.html
29. When baby sleep training goes wrong – the risks of controlled crying: http://www.pinkymckay.com/when-baby-sleep-training-goes-wrong-the-risks-of-controlled-crying/
30. When baby sleep training goes wrong – the risks of controlled crying: http://www.pinkymckay.com/when-baby-sleep-training-goes-wrong-the-risks-of-controlled-crying/

31. Screaming to sleep, Part Two: The moral imperative to end cry it out: http://www.phillyvoice.com/screaming-sleep-moral-imperative-end-cry-it-out/
32. Screaming to sleep, Part Two: The moral imperative to end cry it out: http://www.phillyvoice.com/screaming-sleep-moral-imperative-end-cry-it-out/
33. Babywise advice linked to dehydration, failture to thrive: http://www.aappublications.org/content/14/4/21
34. Dr. Ferber Revisists His 'Crying Baby Theory: http://www.npr.org/templates/story/story.php?storyId=5439359
35. Relationships among infant sleep patterns, maternal fatigue, and development of depressive symptomatology: http://www.ncbi.nlm.nih.gov/pubmed/16128972
36. The emergence of salivary cortisol circadian rhythm and its relationship to sleep activity in preterm infants: http://www.ncbi.nlm.nih.gov/pubmed/10762284
37. Development of fetal and neonatal sleep and circadian rhythms: http://www.ncbi.nlm.nih.gov/pubmed/14505599
38. Great Things About Babywearing by The Babywearer: http://www.thebabywearer.com/index.php?page=bwgreatthings
39. Normal Prolactin Levels in Breastfeeding Mothers by KellyMom: http://kellymom.com/bf/normal/prolactin-levels/

40. Normal Infant Sleep by Darcia Narvaez: http://www.psychologytoday.com/blog/moral-landscapes/201303/normal-infant-sleep-night-nursings-importance
41. Childhood and Society by Erik Erikson: http://www.amazon.com/Childhood-Society-Erik-H-Erikson/dp/039331068X/ref=sr_1_4?s=books&ie=UTF8&qid=1341605352&sr=1-4&keywords=erik+erikson
42. Non-Reactive Cosleeping and Child Behavior: Getting a Good Night's Sleep All Night, Every Night: http://www.thebabywearer.com/index.php?page=bwgreatthings
43. Long Term Cognitive Development in Children with Prolonged Crying: http://www.thebabywearer.com/index.php?page=bwgreatthings
44. Brazy, J E. (1988). Journal of Pediatrics. Mar 112 (3): 457-61. Duke University. Retrieved July 8, 2012, from http://www.thebabywearer.com/index.php?page=bwgreatthings
45. Ludington-Hoe SM. (2002). Case Western U, Neonatal Network. Mar; 21(2): 29-36. Retrieved July 8, 2012, from http://www.thebabywearer.com/index.php?page=bwgreatthings
46. Maternal Behavior as a Regulator of Polyamine Biosynthesis in Brain and Heart of Developing Rat Pups: http://www.thebabywearer.com/index.php?page=bwgreatthings

47. Incubated in Terror: Neurodevelopmental Factors in the Cycle of Violence: http://www.thebabywearer.com/index.php?page=bwgreatthings
48. The Experience-Dependent Maturation of a Regulatory System in the Orbital Prefrontal Cortex and the Origen of Developmental Psychopathology: http://www.thebabywearer.com/index.php?page=bwgreatthings
49. Interview With Dr. Allan Schore, Ghosts From the Nursery: http://www.thebabywearer.com/index.php?page=bwgreatthings
50. Selective Depression of Serum Growth Hormone During Maternal Deprivation in Rat Pups: http://www.thebabywearer.com/index.php?page=bwgreatthings
51. Children with Serious Illness: Behavioral Correlates of Separation and Solution: http://www.thebabywearer.com/index.php?page=bwgreatthings
52. Endocrine and Immune Responses to Separation and Maternal Loss in Non-Human Primates. The Psychology of Attachment and Separation: http://www.thebabywearer.com/index.php?page=bwgreatthings
53. The Mother-Infant Interaction as a Regulator of Infant Physiology and Behavior: http://www.thebabywearer.com/index.php?page=bwgreatthings
54. Control of Sleep-Wake States in the Infant Rat by Features of the Mother-Infant Relationship:

http://www.thebabywearer.com/index.php?page=bwgreatthings
55. Persistent Infant Crying and Hyperactivity Problems in Middle Childhood: http://www.thebabywearer.com/index.php?page=bwgreatthings
56. The Effect of Excessive Crying on the Development of Emotion Regulation: http://www.thebabywearer.com/index.php?page=bwgreatthings
57. Transition to Child Care: Associations with Infant-mother Attachment, Infant Negative Emotion, and Cortisol Elevations: http://www.thebabywearer.com/index.php?page=bwgreatthings
58. Effects of Early Stress on Brain Structure and Function: Implications for Understanding the Relationship Between Child Maltreatment and Depression: http://www.thebabywearer.com/index.php?page=bwgreatthings
59. The Neurobiological Consequences of Early Stress and Childhood Maltreatment: http://www.thebabywearer.com/index.php?page=bwgreatthings
60. Disorders of Attachment in Infancy: http://www.thebabywearer.com/index.php?page=bwgreatthings
61. Infant feeding methods and maternal sleep and daytime functioning: http://www.ncbi.nlm.nih.gov/pubmed/21059713
62. Do solids help baby sleep through the night?: http://www.ncbi.nlm.nih.gov/pubmed/2672785

63. Weaning of infants':
http://www.ncbi.nlm.nih.gov/pubmed/12765913
64. Fatty acids and sleep in UK children: Subjective and pilot objective sleep results from the DOLAB study – a randomised controlled trial:
http://www.ncbi.nlm.nih.gov/pmc/articles/PMC4263155/
65. Factors related to the age of attainment of nocturnal bladder control: an 8-year longitudinal study:
http://www.ncbi.nlm.nih.gov/pubmed/3763302
66. Siesta in healthy adults and coronary mortality in the general population:
http://www.ncbi.nlm.nih.gov/pubmed/17296887
67. Nursies When the Sun Shines by Katherine Havener: http://nursiesbook.com
68. Childhood sleep duration and associated demographic characteristics in an English cohort:
http://www.ncbi.nlm.nih.gov/pmc/articles/PMC3274336/
69. What is Normal Infant Sleep, Part 1 by Tracy Cassels:
http://evolutionaryparenting.com/normal-infant-sleep-part-i/
70. The No-Cry Sleep Solution by Elizabeth Pantley:
http://www.pantley.com/elizabeth/books/0071381392.php

Made in the USA
Columbia, SC
25 April 2019